BE YOUR OWN

INTERIOR
DESIGNER

BE YOUR OWN
INTERIOR DESIGNER

SIÂN REES

MEREHURST

$\mathcal{I}$ dedicate this book to Peter,
without whose loving support
and inspiration it would never
have been written.

• • •

I would also like to thank Sally
Dominic for all her hard work in
typing my illegible, handwritten
manuscript, Sarah Harmer both for
designing the book and helping me to
assemble all the sample boards
and Sara Colledge at Merehurst for
her enthusiasm and calm reassurance.
Last, but by no means least, I would
like to thank my dear Mother, Father
and brother, David, for all their love,
support and encouragement.

• • •

Designer: **Sarah Harmer**
Editor: **Penelope Cream**
Artworks: **Linda White/Brihton Illustration**
Colour separation by Bright Arts, Hong Kong
Printed in Hong Kong by Midas

First published 1996 by Merehurst Limited,
Ferry House, 51-57 Lacy Road, London, SW15 1PR
Text copyright © 1996 Siân Rees
Reprinted 1997
ISBN 1 85391 634-X

A catalogue record for this book is available
from the British Library.

CONTENTS

SAMPLE BOARDS
AN INTRODUCTION

The sample board is the perfect way to try out ideas, colours and styles without committing yourself to anything.

Sample boards are used by interior designers whenever they design a room scheme, and this 'trick of the trade' is the main principle behind this book.

Making up a sample board before you begin to re-decorate a room will help you to produce a successful scheme every time, without making costly mistakes.

The technique of the sample board is to collect together fabric swatches, paint colours or colour charts, wallpaper samples and pictures cut out of magazines, and to present these on a board in the same proportions that you intend to use them in the actual room.

The sample board is the perfect way to try out ideas, colours and styles without committing yourself to anything. For example, if you are out shopping for fabrics and cannot decide between two or three different designs, instead of taking a gamble and choosing one there and then, ask for a small sample of each fabric to take away with you. Some shops even offer what they call 'returnable samples' of about 1 m (40 in) square; these provide you with a reminder of the colours and patterns used – especially if the fabric has a large repeat pattern. These large samples have to be returned, so make sure that they also give you a small sample to keep for your sample board.

When you have collected a good range of swatches and samples, lay them on the sample board and compare the colours. It is surprising how other samples can affect the look of a fabric or a paint colour. The pink floral fabric that looked so good in the shop might just turn out to clash horribly with the peach carpet that you are going to keep. It is this sort of mistake that we have all made in the past – gone shopping and on impulse bought something that on its own would be delightful, but which does

not go with anything that is already in the room. The result can be a mismatching hotch-potch of colours and styles: an expensive mistake! Interior designing is just like clothes shopping: try never to buy anything on impulse, without thinking how it will complement and contrast with what you already have. If you follow this rule, you can build up a successful look.

OBTAINING SAMPLES

You will find that retailers are surprisingly willing to let you have samples, swatches and catalogues to take away. From their point of view it often means that you choose exactly what you want, which means a satisfied customer rather than an unhappy one who might want to exchange the purchases later on.

FABRICS Whether you buy from a department store, interior design specialist or fabric showroom, you should have no problem getting hold of fabric samples to keep. If the fabric you like has a large pattern repeat and lots of different colours, you should ask for a large 'returnable sample'. You may have to leave a deposit on this. In addition, make sure you take two or three small samples to keep, and ask for pieces cut from various parts of the pattern repeat so that you have a complete set of all the different colours used in the design.

You will probably want to choose samples of two or three different fabrics to take home. Look out for contrasting plain shades, small sprigs or checks from the same collection. Fabric manufacturers usually make up a collection using a variety of 'mix and match' fabrics from the same colour palette, to make it easier for people to choose colours for their design scheme. You do not have to use these, of course; it can be more fun, and perhaps more economical, to find your own alternatives.

There is little point in buying a costly plain fabric just because it is part of a set, when you have seen a cheaper alternative that is the perfect match – but make sure it _is_ the perfect match before you buy it by checking the sample on your board.

If your main fabric has, say, yellow and green in equal proportions and you are not sure which colour you want to highlight, then look for both yellow and green complementary plains, take them home and decide once you have put them on your

sample board. You cannot have too many samples, as the more choice you have the more likely you are to end up with exactly the right colour or design for your scheme.

PAINTS Paints are notoriously difficult to choose. You do not want to be so cautious that your finished scheme looks bland and boring, but, on the other hand, if you are going for stronger colours, it is often better to go for a slightly lighter shade than the one you see on the paint chart, as paint colours become more intense when they are used on all the walls in a room. Perhaps the best advice is to choose your shade from one of the large specialist ranges rather than from a standard, ready-mixed range. That way you have a greater choice and you are more likely to buy just the right shade.

You can usually find paint chart cards to take home at a paint shop or DIY store. Use one of these to compare the possible paint colours with your other samples. Once you have narrowed down the choice to just a couple of colours, buy a sample pot of paint in each colour and try them on a section of wall. Use two coats of paint – letting the paint dry thoroughly between coats – and compare these samples with the colours on your sample board.

Once you have chosen the shade that you think you will use, paint a large piece of card with it and take it around the room. You will see how the colour changes when you are near a window, in daylight or lamp light. When you have made your final colour choice, stick the painted card onto your sample board for future reference.

WALLPAPERS When shopping for wallpaper, the same principles apply as for paint. Ask for small swatches to take home and compare with samples already on your board; narrow down the choice to a couple of favourites. It can be difficult, however, to judge how a patterned wallpaper will look when covering all the walls of a room. There may be room set pictures in the pattern or sample books to show you what the paper looks like in a home setting. Once you have chosen a couple of designs, ask the retailers for as large a sample as they can let you have (they normally have a sample roll from which they will cut a length).

Pin these samples (one at a time) onto your wall and live with each one for a few days; keep

Never be tempted to buy anything on impulse, without thinking how it will complement and contrast with what you already have. If you follow this rule, you can build up a successful look.

comparing them to your sample board. It is surprising how something you craved in the shop can somehow just look 'wrong' in your home or next to the other swatches on your sample board.

FLOORING About one-sixth of the colour in a room scheme comes from the floor, and, as this will probably be one of your most expensive purchases, it is important to get it right. Try to get hold of a good size sample of carpet or flooring (such as wood planking, ceramic tiles or sisal matting) to test the impression it will make on the room. If necessary, take several samples of the same flooring and put them all together in a block on your sample board. If your local retailer will not let you have a sample, take a note of the name and address of the manufacturer and contact them direct, requesting a sample piece. There may be a small charge but it is worth it in the long run. Alternatively, if you are keeping your existing flooring, always take a small sample of it with you when you go shopping for fabrics and paints, and use a larger piece for your sample board.

FURNITURE AND ACCESSORIES Of course it is not possible to attach actual samples of furniture or accessories to your sample board, but you can get a flavour of their styles and designs by cutting out and sticking catalogue shots onto your sample board. Catalogues are readily available at furniture stores or by mail order. Look out for advertisements in the

back of home-interest magazines. Even if the example is not the exact piece of furniture or accessory that you will buy, look for something which is similar. From the sample board examples you will soon get the feel for whether you want — for instance, contemporary wrought-iron furniture or something in period-style limed oak. The same goes for accessories: keep an eye out for vases, pictures, frames, china and glass in magazines. Cut out the pictures and use them to fill in spaces on your sample board, just as you would use them in your room.

SOURCES OF INSPIRATION

Your source of inspiration can come from almost anything. At the most simple level, you may be keeping your existing carpet and want to base your colour scheme around it, perhaps sticking to a very simple but co-ordinated colour scheme. Perhaps you are keeping your existing sofa — which may be upholstered in a multi-coloured fabric on which you would like to base your scheme. Or you may have a favourite vase in a particular style or colours which would look perfect translated into a room scheme. Obviously, with items such as a vase, the original source of inspiration cannot be attached to the sample board, so instead try to draw a coloured sketch of the vase on the board, or at least draw in some coloured stripes with crayons to match closely the colours used in the item; always keep the item close to the sample board so that you can refer back to the original colours and style as often as possible.

A theme can also offer inspiration, for example a marine-scape of delicate sea blues and creams, striped deckchair canvas and the faded chalky textures of seashells. Alternatively, it might be the fresh greens of spring that you would like to recreate: sharp citrus shades, complemented by leaf-motif fabrics, wooden furniture and natural accessories. In every case, look for pictures in books, magazines, calendars or catalogues that depict the theme to help you find a starting point.

Another excellent source of inspiration, especially for the beginner, are interiors photographs that you see in magazines. Once you have decided to update a room, start to collect a selection of these completed room schemes torn from magazines: 'tear sheets', as designers call them. When you have

STEP 1

Begin with your source of inspiration — here it is a photograph taken from an interiors magazine — which encapsulates the look you're trying to achieve.

decided on your favourite look, this can be your inspiration. Using a finished room will make it much easier to create a professionally styled scheme, as many of the elements have already been chosen for you. It is then a matter of choosing similar fabrics, paint and furniture to reproduce the look in your own home. If the feature gives details of particular merchandise, make a note of these on your sample board beside the picture, using arrows to indicate what is what. Whatever your inspiration, try to find a reference picture that captures the look, and use this as the central focus for your sample board.

THE WONDERS OF COLOUR

Colour is the element that has the most dramatic effect on a room. It can make the room feel cool, elegant, soothing, stimulating, spacious, warm or even claustrophobic. Colour can change both the 'person-ality' or mood of the room and its apparent size; it is a very powerful tool, so the aim is to make it work <u>for</u> you, not against you.

Interior designers often talk about colour 'theory' and the 'colour wheel' (see overleaf). It sounds daunting, but, in fact, the basics are very simple. Every colour is based on the colours of the rain-bow; red, orange, yellow, green, blue, indigo and violet, plus black and white. To show the relation-ships between all these colours, scientists refer to the 'colour wheel'.

The three 'primary' colours are pure yellow, blue and red, so-called because they cannot be mixed from other colours. All other colours can be made by mixing the three primaries. The three 'secondary' colours are made by adding two pure primary colours: blue and yellow make green, red and blue make violet, and red and yellow make orange.

In between come the hundreds of different intermediate colours, made by mixing different amounts of neighbouring colours. 'Contrast' colours, for example red and green, are those which contrast most strongly and are found directly opposite each other on the colour wheel. Conversely, 'harmonious' colours, for example blue/green, blue and blue/violet, are those that lie next to one another on the colour wheel, and all have one colour in common.

TONES All colours created from those on the colour wheel have the same, strong intensity, but colours found in everyday life, in paints, fabrics and wallpapers for example, also come in different paler tones, or pastels. These are created by adding white to the colour-wheel colours. More muted tones, or 'shades', are created by adding (as the name suggests) black or grey – ie. shadow – to the colour wheel colours.

The 'tone' describes the lightness or darkness of a colour. Take blue, for example. Blue can be any tone from deepest navy to palest sky blue, and a thousand tones in between. At one extreme, the navy tone is created by adding black; at the other end of the spectrum the sky-blue tone is created by adding white. In between are subtle gradations created by adding various degrees of black or white. These are known as 'mid' tones.

Mid tones are very important in colour schem-ing: they link different light and dark colours, which on their own could look rather disparate.

USING THE COLOUR WHEEL FOR ROOM SCHEMES

HARMONIOUS COLOURS Look at the colour wheel and choose three or four colours that lie next to each other. Use these colours to build up a scheme of closely related colours that will create a good 'harmony'. For example, orange, sunshine yellow and lime green colours, or turquoise, cobalt

STEP 2

Stick your 'inspiration' at the centre of your sample board and begin to build up a collection of possible swatches and fabrics around it.

and violet or peach, lemon yellow and raspberry pink. Choose one of the colours at the edge of the group as the accent colour (see below).

CONTRASTING COLOURS For a more lively, contemporary scheme, you could choose colours from opposite sides of the wheel; for example orange, green and violet, or the primaries: red, yellow and blue. The effect can be quite sharp and refreshing and if you use two of the colours – say yellow and blue – for the majority of the scheme, and leave the red for small touches of accent colour, it can work very well.

WARM COLOURS If you have a north-facing or windowless room that needs warming up, go for the warm colours on the colour wheel. These include reds, terracotta shades, oranges, pinks and yellows – perfect if you want to add a splash of sunshine. If you find these strong hues too powerful, stick to softer, more diluted tones such as peaches, raspberry, lemon yellow and pinks; these add warmth without too much intensity. Remember that the closer the shade is to a primary colour, the more powerful it will be – and the more sparingly you should use it.

COOL COLOURS On the opposite side of the colour wheel to the 'warm' colours you will find the 'cool' colours. These include blues, greens and violets – the naturally occurring colours of nature, of water,

STEP 3

As you add more samples to the board, you can reject some in favour of others on grounds of design, colour or price. Constantly refer to the 'inspiration' picture to make sure you keep on the right track.

The colour wheel.

sky and trees. Cool colours have the useful effect of 'drawing back' the walls and making small rooms appear more spacious. The disadvantage, however, is that if used in a north-facing or dark room, cool colours can make the space feel bleak and unwelcoming. In such a case you could 'heat up' the effect with an accent colour from the warm side of the colour wheel, such as yellow or pink.

ACCENT COLOURS Bright touches in the form of trimmings, accessories, flowers and other details can really set off a colour scheme. These splashes of colour are called 'accent' colours. If a room is predominantly one colour, for example green, choose an appropriate accent colour from the other side of the colour wheel, such as terracotta.

If the inspiration for your colour scheme comes from a patterned fabric, then the accent colour may already have been chosen for you if you look closely. For example, if the fabric is predominantly green and yellow with touches of pink, then choose this pink as the accent colour. You may find it more effective to go for a slightly more intense version of the colour for your accent colour, so that it shows up well even in small quantities.

LIGHT AND COLOUR

Different types of light can have a dramatic effect on colour, and, therefore, on interior design schemes. So choosing the right lighting is an important part of

your plan to create the perfect room. When choosing samples of fabrics, wall coverings and flooring, always look at them in daylight, as this gives the best impression of their true colour. But remember that at night the scheme will be lit artificially, so look at the samples by electric light as well.

If the room has large windows and good natural light and is to be used mostly during the day, then it is obviously more important for the scheme to look its best in natural light. If the room – a dining room, or television room for example – is poorly lit or is used mainly in the evenings, then it is more important for the scheme to work well in artificial light.

When choosing samples for your sample board, always look at them in situations as close as possible to your finished scheme. Do this in both natural and artificial light before you make your choice. For example, with lampshade fabric, hold up a piece of sample lit from behind to see the effect of the artificial light. With paint samples, remember that the wall opposite the window will receive direct light and that the paint colour will appear less intense than the wall adjacent to the window; this wall will appear darker, as the only light it receives is reflected light from the other walls. Ceilings will appear darker still as they receive no direct sunlight, so, if you want to effectively 'raise' the height of the ceiling, always choose pure white which reflects the maximum amount of available light. With carpet samples, always lay them on the floor and watch how the colour changes from daylight to artificial light, moving them around the whole room until you are certain that your choice works in all situations.

Remember that several lamps give off a far more attractive light than a single, overhead bulb, which casts an intense pool of light immediately beneath it but produces gloomy shadows elsewhere in the room. Wall lights also create an attractive lighting scheme as most of the beams bounce off the wall and are indirectly reflected into the room. Unless you already have wiring for wall lights, however, having the electrical supply channelled into the wall and replastered can be an expensive business. If the cost is prohibitive, a good alternative is a number of table lamps scattered evenly around the room.

Not all artificial light gives the same effect. The standard light bulb has a tungsten filament which produces a yellowy light. This has the effect of emphasizing the reds and yellows in a decorative scheme, by intensifying these colours and making them appear warmer. This is why a number of table lamps with tungsten light bulbs work well in an evening room where warm colours have been used.

Fluorescent lights have a very harsh light which seems to reduce the intensity of all colours. This is an unflattering choice for both your décor and your guests, unless used judiciously, usually in a concealed position. Low-voltage halogen lights offer a better alternative, producing a white light that is as near to natural daylight as is possible artificially. Halogen is therefore best for rooms that have a fresh, cool colour scheme which looks good in natural light but not in the yellow light of tungsten.

COLOURS FOR DIFFERENT ASPECTS

You should think carefully about how your colour scheme will be affected by the 'aspect' of the room – ie. is it a sunny, south-facing room or a cool, north-facing room? In general it is a good idea to try to warm up a north-facing room by using colours from the warm side of the colour wheel; these include yellows for a sunny look, pale pinks and peaches for a soft, delicate warmth, or hotter terracottas, oranges and crimsons for a stronger effect.

STEP 4

Once you have a good selection of patterned fabrics, start to add plain, complementary shades and tones, pictures of lighting, carpeting and accessories and paint swatches to see how your room will look.

In a south-facing room, you will have plenty of sunlight. You can use any colour scheme in such attractive conditions, but you may feel on a hot summer's day that warm colours are too cloying and claustrophobic. This is a situation where you can use cool colours, such as greens, blues and lilacs. The sunlight will prevent the colours from being too bleak or cold, and will instead produce a fresh, clean feel. You might like to consider using pure white voile at the windows, to diffuse the intense sunlight.

USING PATTERNS AND PLAINS

The task of choosing and working with patterned fabrics and other designs for your room scheme can be daunting. Before wondering 'Just where do I start?', here are a few basic design rules that will help you on your way to the perfect room scheme.

FLORALS The use of floral fabrics, particularly large-scale, multi-coloured designs, can make or break your room scheme. So great is the impact of these designs that it is safest to begin with such fabrics as your starting point. You may decide to keep an existing floral sofa or expensive pair of curtains, or you may fall in love with a particular floral fabric that you have seen in a magazine or a showroom. In either case, this should be the main focus of your sample board. Stick a large cutting of the fabric in the centre of your board and base your whole scheme around it, constantly referring back to it before selecting any further samples.

Take a careful look at your chosen floral fabric and note the proportions of the colours used. If the background colour is a neutral or light shade this is a good basis for the largest surface area in the room – ie. the walls. Use the secondary colour of the fabric – usually a mid-tone – for other elements, for example upholstered furniture, cushions, or a bedspread, and then choose one of the minor but strong, prominent colours for your accent colour. So, for instance, if the fabric has bright yellow- and blue-coloured roses with emerald green leaves on a white background, a successful bedroom scheme might include yellow and white striped walls, a plain blue armchair, the floral fabric for curtains and a blue and white check bedspread with the floral fabric for cushions, edged with emerald green piping.

As you can see from this example, you can add stripes and checks to your scheme, as long as the colours used are taken from your main floral fabric. You can even add another floral, but only if you feel very confident that it will work, and only if the second floral choice is on a much smaller scale than your main floral fabric and preferably in just one colour on white. If not, it will begin to 'compete' with the main floral fabric used, rather than enhance it. Your sample board will help you enormously in judging if the colours and proportions *will* work; if they do not work on the sample board, they will not work in the room scheme.

TOILE DE JOUY In recent years toile de Jouy fabrics have become deservedly popular. These delicate fabrics feature country scenes in one colour on white or cream; red or blue designs are most popular, but you can also buy black, green and yellow versions. Toile de Jouy offers a charming pattern without intense colour and it can be used in a variety of ways. In one of the most attractive but failsafe forms, the same toile can be used as wallpaper for the walls and as matching fabric for curtains, cushions and soft furnishings relieved perhaps by just a sofa and chairs in plain cream upholstery fabric. Far from being overpowering, the effect is very light and airy as the main colour is predominantly white, and yet looks sophisticated and professional as it presents such a co-ordinated look

CHECKS AND STRIPES As we have seen in the previous examples, checks and stripes provide the perfect foil to many patterned fabrics, including multi-coloured florals, monochromatic florals or toile de Jouy. They also 'lift' plain fabrics and walls. Perhaps because of their versatility, checks and stripes are a popular choice with interior designers. Be aware of the different sizes of checks and stripes on offer: they can drastically alter the look of a scheme.

At one end of the scale ginghams are perfect for smaller soft furnishings such as café curtains, contrast linings, cushions, lampshades and fabric-covered boxes. Also look out for the many delightful small-scale check wallpapers that are readily available. In the middle of the range, medium-size checks are useful for small pieces of furniture, throws, bedspreads and bedheads, while the largest checks (5 cm [2 in] or more) are best reserved for sofas, roomy armchairs and large window treatments. You can also use big painted checks in two colours to great effect in a large, airy room.

The same basic principles apply to stripes, from the finest ticking stripes to the broadest marquee stripes. Keep the broadest stripes for walls and large pieces of furniture that will make a real statement. Deckchair stripes are more versatile and can be used almost anywhere, whereas fine ticking stripes are perfect for the smallest surfaces or perhaps where you just want the subtlest suggestion of pattern, say, on the walls of a small room. When using checks and stripes, remember that the impact they make also depends very much on their colour; for instance, 5 cm (2 in) red and white check walls will have greater impact than 10 cm (4 in) lemon and white check walls.

PERFECT PLAINS Never underestimate the power and effectiveness of good, plain fabrics, flooring and walls. The best foil for busy patterns, plains can transform an over-fussy room scheme into a stylish, classic one.

Plains are also a good choice if you are lacking in confidence; for example, you may have found the fabric you want to use but it is a multi-coloured floral and you do not know where to go next. If in doubt, stick with plains, selecting colours from the original fabric. If it is multi-coloured, you will have a number of possibilities from which to choose.

You probably won't need more than two or three plains to complete the scheme. If you stick to plain shades taken from your patterned fabric in this way, you will not go far wrong, particularly if you use the darkest, most intense colours for the smallest areas, and the lightest colours for the largest areas, such as the walls and flooring.

Some of the most plain and simple colour schemes are surprisingly effective: for example, a 'natural' room scheme of plain, honey-coloured walls, cream sofa and chairs and simple Shaker-style furniture. The finished effect has a timeless elegance by virtue of its simplicity. Replace any of the plains with a busy pattern and the effect would be lost.

A similarly successful scheme is that of plain pastel fabrics in ice-cream pink, baby blue, and shades of lemon and mint against cream walls. It is important to use the same tones of colours in this scheme — a shade that is too bright will knock the whole design

off balance. This is where the sample board comes into its own again. By building up your components on a small scale first, you can immediately spot the rogue sample that could destroy the overall effect of the scheme, before you have spent a single penny.

TEXTURAL CONSIDERATIONS

If you have decided to design a room scheme from chic, contemporary plains, it is well worth investigating the use of textured surfaces for adding interest. If you are thinking in terms of a 'natural' room scheme with lots of creams, white and beige, then textures are particularly important. Fortunately, there is a good range on offer.

For fabrics you have the choice of hessian, slub cotton, linen, damask, voile and even velvets. For floors you have the choice of wood, slate, terracotta tiles and flagstones, sisal, coir matting and wool/sisal blends. Furniture designers offer wrought-iron, wood, chrome and raffia, while accessories are made in parchment, wire, glass, wood and papier-mâché.

For walls the choice includes raw plaster, tongue-and-groove panelling and brick, plus all the broken paint effects that add interest: colourwashing, dragging, stamping, stencilling, checks and stripes. How much texture you use is up to you: in general, the plainer your colour scheme, the more successful the use of texture. It is best to avoid using textures with floral patterns, as the look can get very fussy.

With such a huge choice it's easy to be daunted, but don't be — use your sample board, and you'll be delighted by what you will achieve.

Good luck!

APPLE FRESH BEDROOM

The inspiration for this restful bedroom was the Raoul Dufy print of Paris with its impressionist sky of lavender blues, and the green trees representing the spring-time parks around the Eiffel Tower. The colour scheme is perfect for a bedroom; it is peaceful, relaxing and calming without being too cool. The blues have been chosen particularly for their lavender shades which add warmth. The room is east facing, so the sun floods through the window in early morning; this also has the effect of warming the palette of fresh green and blue colours. If the room had been north facing and the colours just that bit cooler, the sunny feeling could have been lost. This shows how important it is to consider the aspect of your room before you choose your colour scheme.

The picture that inspired the colour scheme has also influenced the style of the room. It has a distinctly contemporary look by virtue of the fabrics used; there are no fussy florals, only two-tone checks, an impressionist daisy design and a stylized leaf fabric. Elsewhere lines are simple, with just the subtle 'wave' theme repeated in the window pelmet, tea tray, lamp base, sheet edging, wrought-iron stand and a modern vase. Repeating a theme in this way is a favourite trick of designers, and adds a professional look to the room.

PAINTING THE RIGHT PICTURE

If you are using a picture as the inspiration for a room scheme, hang it in good light in the room to be decorated. Position your sample board beside or near to the picture. This way you can constantly compare and contrast samples both with each other and with your primary inspiration, the picture itself. When referring to the picture, you do not have to follow slavishly the colour proportions used, but if you are unsure of your own sense of style and colour and you find the picture particularly pleasing, you can be very successful if you follow the painter's lead. Here the fresh leaf greens, warm sky blues and purple highlights of the painting have been translated into a room scheme of colour-washed green walls and leafy fabrics, plus accents of blue and purple.

Even the Eiffel Tower is represented by the small wooden table, whose sweeping cross-over legs resemble the elegant arches of the tower depicted in the picture immediately above. The wave theme that is repeated in accessories and details throughout the room is inspired by the artist's open, child-like depiction of clouds.

CHOOSING A BED

The bed is the focal point of any bedroom and the success of this one lies in its colour – a washed cream, which is very easy on the eye. Buying a bed is a big investment, so before you buy, do shop around. Your sample board can help you with this. Make a collection of pictures of beds in magazines, advertisements and catalogues, along with a note of sizes and prices. Then make a short list and go along with a friend or your partner to test your final choice at least twice before you buy.

If you like the design used here, but cannot find anything similar yourself, a good alternative is to buy a simple wooden frame bed and ask a carpenter or joiner to make up a pine foot and headboard and screw them to the bed frame. If your joiner has the right tools, he will be able to do basic cut-out diamond squares or circle designs in the pine to decorate it. If not, you can paint in some 'cut-out'

The restful colour scheme for this room comprises lilac, lavender blues and sharp citrus greens, easily combined in their various shades and tones.

designs yourself, using a paint colour that matches that used on the walls.

When the bed frame is complete, you can achieve a white-washed effect using cream matt emulsion paint. Dilute the paint one to four with water, then apply it evenly using a 5 cm (2 in) paintbrush, following the grain of the wood.

You will find that the milky paint is soon absorbed by the wood and dries quite quickly to leave a white-washed effect, with the natural grain of the raw pine showing through. You may need to give the bed head two or three coats to obtain the desired effect, being sure to let it dry thoroughly between coats.

When you are finished, and are happy with the paint coverage, use a fine-grain sandpaper to rub off the paint very gently in places that would naturally receive more wear and tear – the corners of the foot and headboards, for instance. This gives the completed bed frame a slightly aged effect. To create the cut-out design of the bed shown here, paint the headboard with six small diamonds to represent cut-outs made in the wood. To do this, cut a small card template into a diamond shape and hold it against the bedhead. Draw around the template with a pencil, spacing the diamonds evenly across the bedhead.

When you have drawn in all six diamonds, use a fine artist's watercolour brush to fill in the shapes with the same paint that was used on the walls. Repeat the pattern of diamonds on the footboard as well if you wish. You may need two or three coats to achieve a solid colour effect on the diamond shapes.

DESIGNER BEDLINEN

To give plain bedlinen a designer look, give it a decorative design detail with a scalloped fabric border. Use a washable fabric so that the border fabric does not shrink when the sheets and pillow-cases are laundered.

When choosing the fabric, go back to your sample board to check which samples go with your other choices. Since many upholstery fabrics are dry clean only, you will find a greater selection among dress fabrics (these are usually washable). Choose

Old wooden apple boxes, painted cream, and an ample bedding chest provide useful storage.

Checks have a fresh, bright, contemporary feel — look out for those that combine the various shades of your colour scheme.

samples that have similar colours and styles to your choice of furnishing fabrics and put them on your sample board for easy comparison.

It is best to choose a fabric that can be used any way round, to avoid having to make a join — to edge a double sheet, for instance. Checks, plain chambray or small-sprigged washable dress fabrics are ideal. Buy the same length of fabric as the width of your sheet, plus 10 cm (4 in) for turnings. This should be enough to edge a double flat sheet, four pillowcases and a small cushion. The finished border should be about 12.5 cm (5 in) deep to get the right look.

Make a card template of a 'scallop', drawing round a large coffee cup to form an even curve and cutting it out with sharp scissors. Make sure that the size of the repeated scallop fits exactly into the length of bedlinen: half scallops do not look neat. Lay the template, straight edge to straight edge, on your chosen fabric, and draw round the scallops with dressmaker's chalk. Keep moving the template along the fabric edge until you have completed the edge. Carefully cut out the fabric edge. Repeat the process until you have two matching scalloped lengths of fabric.

Place the scalloped lengths right sides together, and pin then tack so that the scallops match all the way along. Carefully machine stitch the two lengths together 12 mm (½ in) from the edge following the scalloped edge. Snip the outside edges of the scallops. Turn the fabric right side out and press. Press the straight edges under by 12 mm (½ in). Machine stitch the turned straight edges of the border to the front and back edges of the sheet, ensuring that the finished border looks the same on both sides of the sheet. Repeat for the pillowcases.

For a simpler finish which is almost as effective, you could simply add straight-edge borders to your sheet and pillowcases – without the scalloping.

A practical tip for dressing a bed is to use a flat sheet beneath a duvet, especially for a guest bedroom when the guests often stay for just one night. To remake the bed, you then only have to launder the flat sheet and not the whole duvet cover.

MAKING A COVERLET

Quilted bedspreads and comforters are expensive to buy and time-consuming to make, so instead you can make your own simple, double-sided coverlet. These are useful both for decorating the bed, particularly in the guest bedroom, and also for providing a little extra warmth on cool nights.

To make your own, select a suitable fabric. If you have edged your sheet and pillowcases, you can use the same fabric again for one side of the coverlet, although you may be restricted by the width if you used a 115 cm (45 in) wide dress fabric. It is best to stick to the same colour palette as your other bedlinen. Checks complement almost anything from florals to plains. Here two checks are used, one to match the sheet and pillowcase border, the other a larger check designed in colours that perfectly match the blue shades already collected together on the sample board.

Lighting is very important in a bedroom. Avoid harsh, overhead pendant lights. For your bedside lamp, choose a dark lampshade to create a subtle, moody atmosphere after dark.

𝒟 ECORATIVE WINDOW PELMET

f your bedroom window is partly obscured by greenery, and you want to let in as much light as possible, make a simple, decorative pelmet instead of curtains.

STEP I

Buy enough fabric to cover the width of your window, including any architraving. If you have a very large window – more than the width of furnishing fabric (usually 140 cm [54 in]) – choose a fabric that can be used horizontally, such as an abstract, check or plain fabric, to avoid visible joins in the fabric. As with all fabrics for a room scheme, try it out on your sample board before making the final decision.

Having selected fabrics for the front and reverse of the coverlet, measure and cut out two rectangles to fit the bed, keeping the fabric at full width and using the selvedge for turning. Allow about 5 cm (2 in) extra on the length, plus 12 mm (½ in) for turnings. Machine stitch the two rectangles together along the two short sides, right sides facing. Turn right side out and press.

To decorate the coverlet with a designer finish, buy some co-ordinating furnishing fringing, trying various samples against the other fabrics on your sample board first. Stitch the fringing to each longer side of the coverlet, turning in the selvedges for a neat finish as you go. If you prefer one side of the throw to the other, make sure you stitch the fringing to this side for a properly finished look.

When not in use, you can fold or drape the coverlet decoratively at the end of the bed or even on a bedroom chair nearby.

VERSATILE FOOTSTOOL

A footstool can be an alternative coffee table, perfect for hiding piles of magazines, or a bedside table for breakfast in bed. Companies offer footstools in every size and shape. As they are so versatile, you need only change the height of the legs (you can buy a variety of different feet and legs from good hardware stores) and suddenly your footstool becomes a piano stool, a dressing table stool or a luggage rack.

To decorate your footstool you can unscrew the legs and paint them with oil-based eggshell paint. To cover with fabric, use a heavy-duty upholstery staple gun which you will find at most DIY or hardware stores. Lay the fabric in position over the padded stool, turn it over and staple the fabric to the frame on the underside. It is easier if you get someone to help you, so the fabric does not slip around while you are stapling it.

A large display of greenery can make an impressive focal point. Save on money by using greenery from your garden - then just add a flash of colour with a few shop-bought blooms.

STEP 2

Buy some double-sided adhesive card, available from haberdashery suppliers or department stores and specially designed for making decorative pelmets. The card has pattern designs for the shape of the pelmet marked on the reverse. Buy enough to cover the width of your window and architraving, plus 15 cm (6 in) on either side in case you need to centre a printed pattern at the window.
Peel off one side of the backing paper and carefully lay the adhesive card onto the back of the fabric. Smooth away any air bubbles. If the fabric starts to go askew, peel it away from the adhesive card and reposition it correctly.

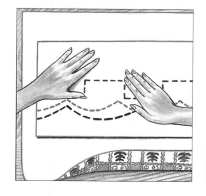

STEP 3

Choose a pattern from the variety of designs printed on the backing paper. Following your chosen pattern, cut through both the card and the fabric stuck to the front. Remember to centre the design over the area of the window frame: this may sometimes mean trimming the edges at both sides.

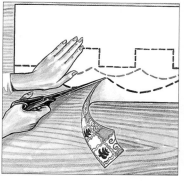

STEP 4

Peel off the reverse backing paper, then position the pelmet against the window architrave. When straight and centred, press it into position. The adhesive is strong enough to hold the pelmet firmly in place. Do not stick the pelmet directly to your walls as it may take off the plaster when you try to remove it.

NEW ENGLAND BEDROOM

*T*he inspiration for this pretty, country-style, New England bedroom comes from the antique hand-stitched samplers above the bed. They have a naive charm and are pleasingly traditional. If, instead of pictures, you would like to hang a couple of hand-stitched samplers on your bedroom walls, for that authentic 'handed-down-from-Grandma' look, then this style is for you.

This look originally came from the American settlers who built new homesteads in a land of plenty and filled them with the plumpest, hand-stitched quilts and the welcoming glow of native cherrywood.

Taking the colours of these hand-stitched samplers as the basis for the colour scheme, the palette is of soft pinks, grey, sage green and cream. It is important to keep to slightly weathered, soft tones, and to steer away from over-clean or sharp shades that would shatter the age-old appeal of the look. If the finished effect is one that looks as if it has been there for many years, then it is a success.

SETTING THE STYLE

This scheme is perfect for those who live in a cottage – or would like to. The small, leaded window, the stripped wooden floor and wood panelling all add to that cosy farmhouse feel. If your room does not have these elements as authentic features, you can always add them. You can even buy self-adhesive lead strips to create fake leaded windows in diamond or square patterns. If you have just moved into a period property, lift up the carpets to see if there are reasonable floorboards beneath. If not, reconditioned old boards are readily available from reclamation companies.

In terms of colour, soft pastels are ideal for a bedroom; they are very gentle to wake up to. If you find pink too fussy, try cream, yellow or pastel blue, all in gentle, time-worn shades. It is a good idea to consider how you might like to change the look later on. Here, for instance, just changing the soft furnishings and repainting the tongue-and-groove panelling would dramatically alter the look of the whole room, with little upheaval.

TONGUE-AND-GROOVE PANELLING

If you have poor-quality plaster walls, or slight damp (unfortunately all too common in old houses with no damp-proof courses), tongue-and-groove panelling can offer a neat improvement. It also provides the perfect effect for a New England-style room, and is practical if you have young children who like to ride around the house on tricycles. It is a fairly simple job to install tongue-and-groove panelling as it slots together very easily and is readily available from DIY and timber merchants in a variety of sizes and widths. As a general rule, the larger the room, the wider the panelling you should choose. Always combine tongue-and-groove panelling with a dado rail and skirting boards to ensure a neat, professional finish.

When building up your sample board, obtain a small sample of tongue-and-groove panelling and paint it to see how it will look combined with the other elements of the room.

If you have inherited a room already clad with tongue-and-groove panelling, but which has been treated with shiny varnish, it is very easy to give it a stylish cottage look with a coat of paint. Lightly sand down the shiny top coat of varnish to create a 'key' for good paint adhesion. You will need a couple of coats of oil-based eggshell paint for good, even coverage. Eggshell is a good option as, being oil-based, it is more durable and you can scrub it clean. However, if you are painting over new tongue-and-groove panelling, emulsion paint will suffice in a room that receives little wear and tear.

WALLPAPER IDEAS

Combining tough, durable panelling with pretty wallpaper creates a good contrast, as the finished effect is very much in the style of an authentic New England room: very homely and yet practical at the same time. This look works best using small-sprigged design wallpaper with a naive, almost hand-painted quality. It is important to choose exactly the right colour and scale of design to complement the room scheme. If the design is too small, the sprigs will not be seen properly; if it is too large, they take on a blowsy, Victorian look which is not right for this New England style. When collecting samples of wallpaper for your sample board, it is a good idea to pin the designs up against the wall itself and then walk away to see how they look from the middle of the room. The bigger the room, the larger the sprigs can be.

As for colour, make sure the wallpaper and your paint are a good match. It is generally easier to start by finding the right wallpaper as you will certainly be able to find a paint colour to match it.

If a hand-stitched sampler is the inspiration for your scheme, go back to it with your wallpaper swatches to find which colours work best before you buy. When calculating the number of rolls of wallpaper you need, measure the surface to be covered, then take the measurements to your wallpaper supplier; they usually offer rolls in a standard width and length, though some more expensive wallpapers may be wider. Remember to allow extra for pattern matching and trimming. Always select rolls of wallpaper bearing the same batch number to avoid colour discrepancies. Consult the manufacturer's charts for the type of adhesive to use.

The colours for this room scheme are those found in the curtain fabric – soft, dusky pinks teamed with sage green and cream.

WASHED-WOOD FLOOR

People have been painting wood with water-based paints for generations and it is a style that translates well to wooden flooring. But instead of using a thick layer of opaque paint, which completely disguises the wood grain, this floor has been painted with a diluted wash of colour, so that all the pattern and grain of the wood is still visible, as with a stain.

First clean and strip your existing floorboards. Do this in a well-ventilated room using an industrial floor sander which you can hire from a tools/equipment specialist or DIY centre. It is cheaper, per hour, to borrow one over a weekend, and this also gives you a chance to take regular breaks.

Remove any protruding nails and repair or replace any old, split boards. When sanding, work in a well-ventilated room and wear a face mask. Follow the hire company booklet on how to get a professional finish. In general, you start with a rough-grade sanding head and graduate to a fine grade to finish. When the sanding is complete, vacuum up all the wood dust and wash down the boards with a 1 to 20 mixture of vinegar and water. Then let the boards dry thoroughly.

Before you begin to paint or dye your floorboards, practise on a few samples first to see which effect you prefer, and to perfect your technique. When dry, compare each one and select your favourite for the sample board. See how well it goes with the other elements you have selected for the room scheme. Is it too light or too heavy? When you are happy with the effect, make a note of the dilution ratios and brushes, so that you can repeat the effect later.

Pale colours such as soft blues, greens and cream work well over light floorboards, such as those cut from pine. Remember that whatever colour you choose, the effect will be greatly diluted once colourwashed over the boards.

There are several ways to add colour to your newly sanded boards. The first way is to use a diluted emulsion paint solution, prepared by mixing one part paint to four parts water. Apply this generously over the boards and work it in with a large decorating brush, brushing in the direction of the grain. Start in a far corner and work your way

The simple lines of this wooden bed add an air of elegance.

back towards the door. The emulsion lightly stains the wood, but the coloured layer is transparent enough for the wood grain to show through.

For a deeper colour, paint over the boards again in the same way. Conversely, to expose more of the wood grain, wait 5–10 minutes, then gently wipe over the surface with a clean, damp cloth, in places, to remove some of the surface paint.

If you want the finish to be hardwearing, you will need to varnish it. Before you apply the varnish, lightly sand over the surface, then brush with sanding sealer to prevent the varnish from soaking into the colourwashed wood and darkening it. Use two coats of matt oil-based varnish. Note that polyurethane varnish will make the finish slightly yellow in colour.

Alternatively, you can use a general-purpose clothes dye to add colour to your floorboards. Mix up some powdered dye with water and paint it over the floor using a large paintbrush; finish with varnish as before. The wood will absorb the dye, and the effect is less milky than using a diluted emulsion wash. The treatment used on the floorboards shown here is a pale grey-blue emulsion which is the perfect foil for the pink walls. The boards have been left unvarnished, so that they will wear gradually in an authentic, distressed way.

Look for small, sprigged-design fabrics which are perfect for this style. Archive designs, taken from historical designs, offer a particular charm.

FINE FURNITURE

The homely, traditional look of this room means that the bed is the focus of attention. A bed with a simple curved headboard in warm pine or American cherry is just right. If you cannot afford cherrywood, but like the rich colour, use a wood stain and polish to transform a pine bed frame. Once again, try out the effect in a place where it will not show – on the reverse of the headboard, for instance – before you go ahead. It is a good idea to give other furniture in the room the same treatment.

If you want unadorned, New England styling, you can transform the whole character of an existing chest of drawers or bedside table by replacing large Victorian 'bun' handles with neat, Shaker-style knobs.

A rocking chair is a must for this New England bedroom. Again, authentic cherrywood examples are costly, so think about buying a second-hand pine chair and giving it a covering of cherrywood stain, or perhaps painting it a plain matt cream colour using oil-based eggshell paint.

TIME FOR BED

For bedlinen, you can mix patterns to your heart's content, as long as they are all of the same colour palette and scale. Simple checks, ginghams and fine stripes are best for this look, as well as tiny floral prints, but avoid anything that is fussy or frilly. Sheets, blankets and quilts are very much the order of the day – forget the modern-day duvet, it just does not convey the right kind of mood.

To mimic an authentic homestead bed, pile on one or two American-style quilts. These days antique ones are much sought after and are expensive, so look out for reproductions. Simple geometric designs are most appropriate, such as the star shape, or traditional motifs, such as the school house, symbolizing the virtues of simple village life, or the basket representing plenty. Alternatively, you could go to your local soft furnishing specialist and get a quilt made to order. Select a floral or sprigged outer fabric and a candy-striped lining, so that the comforter can be reversed.

Hearts were a popular folk art motif in early American homes. They adorn many things from quilts and furniture to sets of hooks, as here.

$\mathcal{S}$IMPLE-SEW CURTAINS

Before making your final fabric selection, try out a few pieces on your sample board to see which one goes best with the other elements in the room.

Do not forget a colourful heap of pretty cushions to finish dressing the bed. You could sew some yourself using remnants of fabric left over from the curtains or comforter, or look out for cushion covers in antique shops. Finally, hand-stitch 'Home Sweet Home' on a plain white cushion using simple cross-stitch in pink thread, tracing it out with pin pricks or dressmaker's chalk first.

FINISHING TOUCHES

Final details are important for any room and for this look they should have a home-made quality. If you would like to have a go at patchwork, begin with something small at first, like a cushion, to see how you get on before embarking on a quilt. Begin by collecting some fabric remnants from your local haberdashery store, as these are very cost effective. Patchwork quilting is an art in itself, but it is also a question of having enough time and patience. Use paper patterns to create your cushion square and then cut up the fabric pieces to match, adding 12 mm (½ in) all round for turnings.

Simple, hand-stitched samplers are another decorative accessory that you can make yourself, and there are plenty of beginner's kits available. Start with something easy at first, then build up a collection of finished samples and hang them around the walls instead of pictures.

If you are good with your hands, you could go on to make a dried-flower wreath to hang on your bedroom door or wall. Start with a basic wreath made from twigs bent round to form a ring. You can buy these in various sizes from good florists – or even make up one for yourself using willow twigs. Decorate the twig wreath with tiny dried flowers, such as baby's breath (*gypsophila*), pale pink rose buds and *helichrysum*. Work your way around the wreath gluing the dried flowers in place using a glue gun to secure the stems between the twigs.

Dried flowers – rather than fresh arrangements – are better for this style of room. Look for soft pink and grey-green shades, and fill a wicker basket to the brim.

For a tiny cottage window like this that is not over-looked, there is no need to go to the trouble of lining the curtains. Buy a pole about 30 cm (12 in) longer than the width of the window so that the curtains do not overlap the window too much.

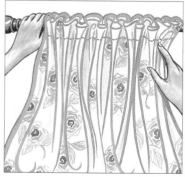

STEP 1

Measure the drop of your windows then add a total of 22.5 cm (9 in) – ie. 5 cm (2 in) for the double hem, 7.5 cm (3 in) for the height of the pole above the window and 10 cm (4 in) for looping the fabric over the pole at the top. Cut two widths of fabric to this length.

STEP 2

Double hem the fabric by 2.5 cm (1 in) at either side and machine stitch. Then turn over the top edge of each curtain by 10 cm (4 in) to form the pole casing. Tack and double hem by machine. Double hem the bottom of each curtain by 2.5 cm (1 in), tack in place and machine stitch.

STEP 3

Slide a 5 cm (2 in) diameter curtain pole through the loop sewn in the top edge, and gather up one curtain to the left and the other to the right. Slot the pole, with the curtains hanging from it, into the wall brackets and screw in place.

SUNSHINE DAYS BEDROOM

*T*he curtain fabric used here provided the inspiration for the room: an impressionist-style design with a yellow background combined with contemporary floral posies in pink, lilac, orange and green. The fabric contains all the colours needed to make the bedroom a pleasure to wake up to.

When using such a mixed palette of colours, look out for one main colour to pull together all the themes. In this case it is the predominantly yellow background of the fabric. Yellow is a cheerful, mood-lifting colour and it is also one of the most versatile colours, complementing and enhancing every other shade you might combine it with.

The secondary colours of the fabric – which include the pinks, oranges and lilacs – are used throughout the room to add contrasting touches of accent tones in the form of soft furnishings and accessories.

As the room is north-facing, the curtains have been lined with a plain peach chintz, which has the effect of warming the quality of the light as it enters the room. Elsewhere this peach theme is repeated in the blanket chest at the end of the bed and the bumble bee stencil on the walls. The sample board provides the basis for achieving the exact balance of colour before you begin.

WALL SHADES

Having established the curtain fabric as the starting point, the walls were painted yellow to match. It is important to select exactly the right shade and to do this the sample board is essential. Attaching a piece of the curtain fabric to the board enables the possible paint samples to be compared with it. Buy tester pots and brush the paint onto small pieces of card, then use these to compare the different shades. Remember that once your whole room is painted, the intensity of the colour will be magnified as the light bounces off the coloured walls. In view of this, it is a good idea to choose a slightly lighter shade – you can always wash over it later with a colourwash solution of one part paint to four parts water using a slightly more intense shade of yellow.

Paint the walls with two coats of vinyl matt emulsion, let them dry off thoroughly then check that you have not missed bits or left patches. Always check the walls in strong daylight, as this is the most revealing light with which to see uneven coverage. For contrast, the dado rail here was painted in a very pale lilac.

To complete the look, the walls above the dado rail are stencilled with peach-coloured bees. Stencilling is an easy way to add decoration to your walls and the great thing is that you do not have to be artistic to achieve exciting and professional effects. One of the more interesting ways to use stencilling is to repeat a simple motif all over a plain painted wall to resemble a sprigged wallpaper as here. It is easiest to place the stencil at random rather than in a strict pattern, as for this you would need to mark out a grid on the walls. The other problem with drawing out a grid is that it assumes your walls are straight, which in older properties is often not the case.

This bumble-bee design was applied using a pre-cut, single-colour, acetate stencil, but you can choose from a vast selection in the shops. If you feel confident enough, you could draw and cut your own stencil design, perhaps taking inspiration from an accessory in the room. Remember that the parts that you cut out will be the parts that create the stencilled image. Try out the design on your sample board before you begin stencilling onto your walls.

Select a colour that is stronger than your walls, or the stencil will not show up. Ideally the design should be clearly visible from the centre of the room, but not glaring. Generally the softer the image, the more professional the effect. Use stencilling crayons applied with a round stencil brush for a neat, quick-drying finish to avoid smudging.

SHELF FEATURE

To add useful shelving for books and accessories, while also creating an attractive feature, painted shelves are used here to create an alcove effect over the bed. Four small shelves fixed on either side of the bedhead and one large shelf running across the whole width of the bed form a frame for a favourite picture.

Curly wrought-iron brackets painted pale lilac are used to support the shelving, which is painted yellow to match the walls. Use a spirit level held against the wall to mark your horizontal lines with a pencil before drilling the bracket holes in position. Make sure that you measure and mark out the position of your picture to ensure that it is exactly centred between the shelves.

You could further enhance the look of the shelving by gluing painted MDF shelf trim to the edges of the shelves using a glue gun, or you could even use a length of fringed trimming, a wallpaper border or strips of fabric as a decorative treatment. In all cases, stick to the same colour palette to avoid an over-fussy effect. Try different alternatives on your sample board first, to check which works best with other elements of the scheme.

CURTAIN CHOICES

Once you have selected your curtain fabric, you need to decide on a treatment that will best set it off. The curtains used here are lined with a plain chintz fabric in a strong peach colour; this choice was tested on a sample board first. It is not an immediately obvious choice, but was in fact selected to create a warm, glowing quality as the sunlight filters through the French windows of this north-facing garden flat. As the room scheme is quite

The main colour for this room scheme is a soft, sunny yellow. It is combined with bright touches of pink, lilac and strong peach, as seen in the curtain fabric.

As long as you keep to the same palette of colours, you can mix a variety of floral fabrics.

If you are unsure about stencilling your own design, choose a subtly-patterned wallpaper instead, perhaps combined with a co-ordinating border.

contemporary, a simple treatment works best. There are no fussy tie-backs, ruches or frills — the only concession to adornment is a row of bows made up in the same peach lining fabric, which are used to tie the curtains to the pole. The lining fabric is a fine chintz that does not fray. This means that it is very easy to create the ties. You could use ribbons in a similar way. If you like the effect of the ties, but feel they are rather impractical (they do make the curtains more difficult to draw), sew on some heading tape, hang the curtains on rings and leave the ties as a decorative feature. The wooden pole was painted with the same yellow emulsion paint as the walls and then finished with a durable coat of satin water-based acrylic varnish.

USING SCREENS

To create a degree of privacy within a room — or to shield a large, uncurtained window from prying eyes — use a screen. You can find these from various sources; many soft furnishing specialists will make up a screen to your precise size and shape with two or three hinged sections. Alternatively, you could search your local junk shop for a solid frame that needs repadding and covering. Or, best of all, you could make one yourself. This is a good idea as the raw materials are very cheap and yet finished screens are expensive items to buy.

Start with two or three matching sections of MDF or plywood. Most DIY centres or timber merchants will cut them to the size you want. If you want a Gothic arch, or a scalloped or curved top, it will cost you more, but any good timber merchant should be able to offer these options – the board simply has to be cut with a jigsaw. Be prepared to take along a paper pattern for them to follow.

Once you have the cut sections, cover the fronts and backs with white polyester wadding. Secure the wadding in place at the edges with staples, using a staple gun. Do not use wadding that is too thick

or the staples will not hold. Cover the sections with your chosen fabric and again secure at the edges with staples at 5 cm (2 in) intervals. Stretch the fabric tight to get a good, professional finish. Finally, glue plain fabric trimming at the edges to cover the staples. Use three brass hinges to join the sections together securely, screwing them in place right through the fabric cover.

For a smart, co-ordinated look for your bedroom, you could cover the screen with a fabric that matches your curtains or bedcover. The fabric used here is different from those seen elsewhere in the room, but it still continues the colour theme as it contains shades from the same colour palette, namely yellow, lilac and green. Tried on the sample board first, the fabric offered a fresh contrast with the other fabrics used in the scheme.

Enhance your colour scheme by choosing complementary-colour flowers. These pretty peach tulips are perfect in a clear glass vase where their bright green stems are clearly visible.

$\mathcal{T}$OP HAT BOXES

You can buy cheap cardboard hat boxes in stationery outlets and good department stores. They come in a range of different sizes and so can be used to store almost anything, from socks or balls of wool, to buttons and children's toys.

To give them designer style and make them into a stunning storage feature, cover these shop-bought cardboard hat boxes with fabric then stack them up in the corner of your bedroom.

FURNITURE FLAIR

This bedroom needed a light, airy, sunny summer's day feel. Any type of plain wood furniture would have been too heavy and overpowering. Pictures collected together for the sample board showed that the look was most effective with expensive-looking, painted furniture. The attractively shaped, ready-to-paint, unvarnished wood bedhead and bedside table came from a local DIY store and so offered a high-style, budget alternative.

To decorate the furniture as shown here, use two coats of cream eggshell paint as the base, and highlight the curved recesses of the bedhead with the same soft lilac shade as that used on the dado rail. The colour difference is just enough to enhance the carved detailing and give the bedhead a more expensive, solid feel without being overpowering

Give the bedside table a similar paint treatment to that applied to the bedhead. In addition, remove the handles and stencil a loose, filigree motif in the same peach colour that was used to stencil the bees on the walls. To achieve the effect shown here, stencil the motif so that the filigree appears to entwine the handles, running around them in a decorative way, providing additional detail. Replace the original handles or substitute small, fine china ones — or any other style that catches your fancy — to complete the transformation.

The dressing table was a lucky junk shop find; it looks wonderful painted in the same yellow as the walls. When painting over wood, remember to switch from water-based emulsion to oil-based eggshell, as emulsion is generally not durable enough for furniture.

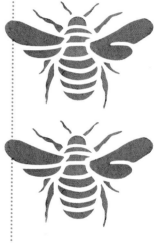

STEP 1

Measure the circumference and the depth of the box. Cut a rectangle of fabric to size, adding 10 cm (4 in) to the depth for finishing. Similarly, measure the circumference and depth of the lid. Cut out another fabric rectangle to this size, adding 10 cm (4 in) to the depth. Place the lid flat on the fabric. Cut out one circle of fabric for the top of the box and another for the bottom of the box.

STEP 2

Glue all round the box and stick on the long rectangle of fabric, leaving a 5 cm (2 in) overlap at the top and bottom edges. Abut the fabric ends at the join, but do not overlap them.

STEP 3

Snip the excess fabric into strips at the bottom and top edges of the box. Neatly fold over these strips and glue down one by one, smoothing out any air bubbles.

STEP 4

Glue the fabric strip to the edge of the lid. Leave a 5 cm (2 in) overlap at the top and bottom edges. Abut the fabric ends at the join, but do not overlap them. Snip the excess fabric into strips at the bottom and top edges of the lid. Neatly fold over these strips one by one, smoothing out any air bubbles. Stick one circle of fabric onto the top of the lid and another over the bottom of the box.

You can create a stunning wallpaper-effect design by repeating a single-colour stencilled motif — such as these bees — over the walls.

37

PAINTED TILE-EFFECT BATHROOM

*T*he inspiration for this design was a friend's bathroom. It had been updated with a fake tile paint treatment using a checkerboard of blue and white eggshell paints that was both easy to copy and highly effective. The bathroom suite was white and period in style but with clean, classic lines, and the accessories had a cheerful look combining gingham checks and folk art detailing. Starting with these basics, it was easy to expand the theme by building up swatches on a sample board.

If you are working to a tight budget, tiling can be prohibitively expensive; the tiles themselves can be costly, and you will need to pay a tiler to put them up, unless you do it yourself. It's a far easier, cheaper and altogether simpler solution to 'paint' your tiles. This not only means that you do not have to go to the bother or expense of tiling, but it also means that you can just repaint them if you tire of the look.

Before you start, you will need to choose the colour of your 'tiles'. Two-tone tiling is very effective, but you can also use three colours or even more. Using cream or white as one of your 'tile' colours is a good way to off-set your second colour choice.

PERIOD PAINTS

You will find that period-style paint collections have exactly the right historical shades for each look, be it Georgian, Victorian or Shaker. This is because manufacturers use historical references to make the colours as authentic as possible.

The paints are often more expensive than standard paint ranges and some will also be made in a traditional manner using old-fashioned ingredients that give them an age-old chalky finish. However, if you cannot afford to pay the extra price but want an authentic look, go to a specialist and bring home one of their colour charts, or, better still, a small sample pot. Attach the colour chart to your sample board, or paint a small section of white card with the paint, leave to dry, and attach that to your sample board. Then refer to the standard paint ranges and look for the closest possible match. Before you buy the paint, compare standard colour charts with the samples on your board until you have narrowed it down to the closest matching shade.

For a bathroom it is best to go for a washable oil-based paint. Both eggshell paint, with its slight sheen, and gloss paint can be most effective for fake tiles. Both these finishes are oil-based so you will be able to wipe down the 'tiles' with soapy water to keep the walls clean.

PAINTED TILE STYLE

The main thing to remember when painting fake tiles is that accuracy is everything. The whole effect will look sloppy and amateurish if you try to cut corners with your preparation.

First paint your walls with the lighter of the two tile colours — here cream has been used. Use two coats to get a good, even finish, and leave to dry overnight between coats.

Next, decide on the size of tile you want to paint — the tiles in this room are 10 cm (4 in) squares, which is a standard size for traditional tiles.

Before you start, check to see if your walls are straight — this is very often not the case in period houses. To do this you will need a plumb line (a lead

weight on the end of a long piece of string). You can make your own or buy one at a hardware store. Then, starting in the far left-hand corner of the wall you are going to 'tile', measure up 60 cm (24 in) from the skirting board (ie. six tiles high), and mark this point tight into the corner. Hold the plumb line up against this mark and follow the line of the plumb line against the wall with a soft pencil. Remove the plumb line and look at the pencil line you have drawn. If it is parallel to the corner, the walls are perfectly straight, but, if not, then the walls are not at right angles to one another at the corner. If this is the case you will need to use your marked line as your starting point in order to 'tile' in straight lines. From this starting point, using a long plastic ruler and a soft pencil, mark out 10 cm (4 in) intervals across the wall until you reach the end. Then, from the same starting point, mark out 10 cm (4 in) intervals down the wall until the whole wall is marked out with evenly spaced 10 cm (4 in) marks.

Check a few of the marks at random to ensure that all the spaces are exactly 10 cm (4 in), then join up all the marks with masking tape to create a grid across the whole wall.

Next, dip a 2.5 cm (1 in) paintbrush into your second paint colour — Shaker blue in this room — and begin painting in the alternate squares, both across and down to create the checkerboard effect. Work from the top left-hand corner across and down to the bottom right-hand corner to avoid smudging. Leave the paint to dry before removing the masking tape.

When the paint is completely dry on all the walls, and the 'tiling' is finished, gently use a soft, clean rubber to erase any visible pencil marks.

If you are putting in a new bath like the one in this bathroom, 'tile' the walls before the bath is fitted.

USING SLATE

Your choice of flooring depends on the function of the room. The look of grey-blue slate tiles suits this bathroom, and, being hard-wearing, these tiles are a practical choice too. On the down side, they are expensive, so look upon them as an investment purchase for a home you intend to spend many years living in. Slate, as with all types of stone flooring, is fairly heavy, so it is best to check with

The period blue — with its distinctive grey undertones — is teamed with cream-coloured walls, cobalt blue accessories and just a touch of soft red for the stencilled heart border.

If you have a cloakroom or second bathroom, you can repeat the painted tile idea — this time from floor to ceiling.

Bright, colourful towels, neatly rolled and placed in woven baskets provide a touch of colour, and mean that clean towels are always near at hand.

a builder or tile specialist that your substrate is strong enough to bear the load. As slate is naturally porous, once laid the tiles must be given two coats of sealant. This deepens the colour and leaves the slate waterproof. Unlike terracotta, however, slate, once sealed, requires no further maintenance. Have the slate tiles professionally laid and sealed by an expert for the best finish.

RENOVATING A BATH

If you are buying a cast-iron, roll-top bath, you have several choices. You can buy a reproduction model that offers the advantages of new technology combined with period styling. Or you could buy an original Victorian bath that has been renovated, although these can be very expensive. Finally, you could go to a reclamation yard and buy a Victorian tub with a view to having it renovated, in which case it is a good idea to get a quote from a specialist bath re-enamelling company first; you could be surprised by the total cost of the bath plus the re-enamelling.

The fun thing about roll-top baths is that you can decorate them on the outside using a variety of paint effects including verdigris, marbling or stencilling. Should you tire of the effect, you can simply paint over it again. Always use waterproof, oil-based paints.

Remember that as the bath is freestanding, the pipes cannot be hidden behind a bath panel or ducting. The pipes have to come out of the adjacent wall, which is not always practical, or straight up through the floor if the bath is in the middle of the room.

HANGING SHELF UNITS

Storage is frequently a problem in a bathroom, and although sleek fitted units may be the solution for a smart, contemporary look, they are out of keeping with this traditional style bathroom.

Instead, one favourite choice is an open shelf unit with leather hanging straps. Look for something similar in pine, and paint it yourself using the same oil-based paint that was used for the tiles. Drill through the wood and fit your own hanging straps made from sturdy leather thongs.

Open shelves are a good solution for storage of attractively packaged skincare products, oils and creams. If you find a bath care range presented in beautiful, coloured glass bottles, you can keep these for ever more, decanting cheaper brands into them when the contents run out. Another alternative is to use old-fashioned drugstore-style bottles.

You will probably also want a proper medicine cabinet with a tight-fastening or locking door. Again, hand-painted hanging cupboards are very expensive, so look for a cheap pine alternative with a simple, stylish shape and paint it to match your painted tiles. First rub the cupboard down using sandpaper, then paint with two coats of oil-based eggshell.

Hook rails can be decorative as well as practical. Use them to hang up flannels, sponge bags, brushes and towels.

CRACKLE GLAZING

This attractive paint effect is created by applying a coat of water-based paint on top of a dry coat of crackle glaze (available from specialist paint suppliers); this causes cracks to develop in the paint surface. Remember that the effect is best seen where the two colours of paint selected are highly contrasting. Here, a light cream colour has been used for the crackle glaze base with a top coat of blue.

STENCILLED BORDER

The heart and leaf border here softens the puritanical lines of the bathroom. Before stencilling onto your walls, test your technique on the sample board. Avoid being too heavy-handed; this can result in an ugly outline of paint around the stencil.

First, decide where you want to position your border decoration. Here it is just above the dado rail and also at picture-rail height, which has the effect of lowering the ceiling. Next select the stencil (this technique uses a pre-cut acetate stencil in two parts, but you can design your own). Lay the first acetate on a protected work surface and lightly and evenly spray the reverse with an adhesive spray. Place the acetate in position flat against the wall so that it sticks in place. Start on the far left-hand side of the wall and work towards the right (if you are left-handed you may want to work in the opposite direction to avoid smudging the paint).

Solid oil crayons, specially designed for stencilling, dry almost instantly, and so prevent smudging. Rub the crayon on an unused corner of the acetate, depositing a thin film of dry oil paint. Then take a small stencil brush and use a circular motion to load it with paint by picking up all the paint onto the bristles until there is none left on the acetate.

Still using a circular motion, move the brush over the stencil, depositing a fine layer of paint on the wall. Lift off the acetate and move along to the right. Line up the repeat marks as you move along and continue stencilling. Continue along the whole wall, recharging the paint brush as necessary.

Before applying the second colour, clean the brush in white spirit and dry. Then, taking your second acetate, line up the stencil so that the repeat lines on the second acetate overlap the areas already stencilled on the wall. Load your brush with the second paint colour as before and begin stencilling again, just as described previously.

Choose bathroom taps from the wide range of styles available. Remember not to mix gold and chrome fixtures and fittings in one bathroom; stick to one type of metal throughout.

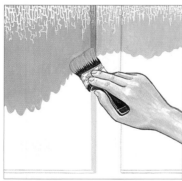

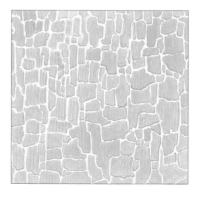

STEP 1
Paint a coat of cream water-based emulsion paint over the surface. Allow to dry and paint with a second coat. Allow to dry once again. Then paint an even coat of crackle glaze over the cream basecoat. The thicker the coat of crackle glaze you paint, the larger the cracks will be. Allow the crackle glaze to dry completely.

STEP 2
Paint the top coat of water-based emulsion paint over the crackle glaze. The paint may be easier to apply if diluted with a little water.

STEP 3
Remember, the cracks will form in the direction in which you brush the paint. Seal with a coat of oil-based varnish. Crackled surfaces must be sealed with an oil-based varnish, not a water-based one.

TULIP TIME BATHROOM

*T*he advent of spring, with its bright yellow daffodils and tulips, inspired the styling of this bathroom. Traditionally this is a time when we turn our thoughts to renovating our homes – to spring cleaning, repainting and updating. It is a very positive, uplifting time of year. In response to this, daffodil yellow and turquoise green are used as the two main colours for this room scheme. For the green colour, the bright leaf green of the tulip plants would have been suitable, but this period house needed something less modern and intense.

By adding a touch of blue to leaf green, the resulting turquoise colour provides a smart and sophisticated look for the panelling, which enhances the room by giving greater weight to the lower half of the wall. This device is useful for adding a feeling of solidity to a room, creating an expensive, elegant look that disguises the use of standard MDF or other budget materials.

The leaf green colour could also have been used to stain the floorboards or selected as a carpet colour, but instead a dark, wooden floor was chosen. This, being darker still than the wall panelling, gives a firm base shade to the room, further enhancing its solid, period-style character.

The room is finished with a row of potted yellow tulips in rough, old terracotta pots and colourful accessories in turquoise and yellow.

ADDING PANELLING

Wooden panelling of any description adds character to a room, and it is a popular way to enhance the period styling of a bathroom. Tongue-and-groove panelling is most often used and this can impart a cottagey look, particularly when painted. Usually light colours are used; cream, white or pastel shades feel right. But in this example, instead of a cosy, cottage look, a grander, townhouse style has been created for an altogether smarter, more sophisticated ambience.

Square, Georgian-style panelling was used to produce this impression .It looks authentic and expensive, but is actually made from rectangular plywood boards nailed over battens, and enhanced by dowelling to create a three-dimensional effect.

A deep, ornate skirting board was added to the bottom, and a moulded, fairly wide dado rail added to the top. These were all painted to match, to further enhance the authentic look of the panelling.

DRAGGED PAINT EFFECT

Once installed, the panelling needed a period-style paint treatment to create the right effect. Historical paint treatments can be very evocative of this era; here, to continue the theme of a Georgian townhouse, dragging was used. This employs a base colour with a slightly lighter or darker tone dragged over the top. Paint effects, which build up layers of colour in this way, create a feeling of quality and depth that is not achievable with flat paint colour alone.

To ensure that the finished paint effect creates the required colour, play with various possibilities on pieces of card. Once you are satisfied that you have the correct colour combination and dragging texture, make a note of the way you achieved the effect and place the card on your sample board. Here, a deep sea green forms the base colour, which is dragged over with pale turquoise. For a waterproof finish, always use oil-based paint for painting wood panelling in bathrooms.

To achieve the dragging effect, first apply two coats of dark green

Mint greens, tulip yellow and touches of orange are the colours central to this spring-time bathroom.

eggshell, leaving it to dry thoroughly between applications. If you are right-handed, start at the top of the panelling, in the corner furthest away from you, and work back towards the door so that you do not smudge the paintwork as you move round.

Using a decorating brush, apply a coat of pale turquoise eggshell paint diluted one part paint to one part white spirit. Paint it on in vertical stripes 60 cm (2 ft) wide, working from the top of the panelling down. Then carefully drag a flogger brush, dampened with white spirit, in smooth, vertical strokes through the wet paint, so that the background colour shows through in fine stripes. Follow the direction of the panelling with your brush strokes, working downwards on the verticals and across on the horizontals. Leave to dry.

To protect the paintwork, if, for example, you have young children who splash about, you could seal the painted panelling with a coat of oil-based varnish, but it tends to add a slightly yellow tinge.

WALLPAPER MADE PRACTICAL

Many people shy away from using wallpaper in their bathrooms thinking it is impractical, when, in fact, it can look extremely smart, particularly in older-style properties. You can buy different grades of wallpaper that are designed to withstand various conditions, including the damp and condensation of steamy bathrooms. At one extreme is tough vinyl, which has a durable coating designed to take regular washing down; then there are spongeable wallpapers and, finally, non-washable wallpapers. The latter have no resilient top coat, but you can render them practical for bathrooms if you paint over them with a proprietary wallpaper glaze; these are available in either eggshell or gloss finishes. A glaze will create a water-resistant barrier to seal the wallpaper from the effects of steam and moisture and also prevents the seam from opening up.

When you are looking for wallpaper samples to build up your sample board, make a note of the types of paper that are water-resistant, as it may influence your decision later. If you are looking for a fairly plain design, as used here, there should be plenty of choice, so it should be quite easy to find a suitable washable or spongeable wallpaper. This means that you will not have to seal it later.

The combination of sunny yellow, turquoise and check curtain fabric makes a stunning colour statement

Small touches make all the difference to the final look of a room. This bathroom is decorated with marine-inspired accessories, including wooden sailing boats, starfish and drift-wood pictures.

Here the chosen yellow wallpaper has a subtle damask-effect pattern. It adds just a touch of texture to the walls and creates an attractive foil for the dragged walls.

SELECTING A SUITE

For this Georgian townhouse look, a period-style suite is the best choice. White is still the best-selling colour and the sales reflect the versatility that this shade gives you, should you want to change your colour scheme at a later time.

The suite used here has attractive moulded detailing that reflects the design of the panelled walls. The shape is smart and traditional without being too fussy or ornate.

Do some window shopping before making any decisions about buying a new suite. Bathroom showrooms often have room sets to help you visualize the completed look. A good specialist bathroom company will also be able to give you advice on any particular installation or plumbing queries you might have.

51

Use pictures from magazines and bathroom brochures on your sample board to help you to identify the styles you like before making any major purchases. If you like the impression of quality that the wood fixtures add to this room, you could update your existing suite by replacing the bath panel with a wooden one and buying a pine toilet seat.

It is also easy to restore or revive old wood. If, for instance, it has been covered in many layers of varnish or paint, you can either take the bath panel to a specialist stripping company, or you can do it yourself.

If you do strip it yourself, make sure that you follow the manufacturer's instructions on the paint stripper container. The chemicals are toxic, so protect your hands with rubber gloves and always work in a well-ventilated room, taking regular breaks.

WINDOW STYLE

As privacy is usually a consideration for bathroom windows, it is often a choice between etched glass or permanently lowered Venetian blinds. For a softer look this bathroom has a Roman blind combined with a stylish, no-draw curtain.

The large, Georgian sash window is a very attractive feature in this bathroom and it would have been a shame to change the glass or hide the window. By using a Roman blind, the window can be revealed most of the time as, with the toilet to one side, privacy is only needed when someone is taking a bath. Yellow fabric gives the south-facing room a cheerful glow, even when the blind is lowered, shutting out the direct light.

The real style statement of the window treatment, however, is produced by the simple curtain. Hung from a pole above the window, it is made

Look for checked fabrics that contain all the colours used in the room scheme – they will bring the look neatly together.

$\mathscr{M}$ AKING A ROMAN BLIND

Roman blinds are more elegant than plain roller blinds. When raised, they fall into deep horizontal folds.

STEP 1

Buy sufficient tape to run from top to bottom of the blind at 30 cm (12 in) intervals, and along each edge, plus 2.5 cm (1 in) extra for turnings; double this amount of cord; enough rings to sew at 15 cm (6 in) intervals along the tape, and one screw eye for every line of tape.

STEP 2

Stitch double 1.5 cm (¾ in) side hems and a 5 cm (2 in) double bottom hem, leaving one end of the hem open. Turn over 3 mm (⅛ in) at the top and sew on touch-and-close tape.

from just one width of unlined fabric, tied in a casual knot at dado-rail height. As the fabric is a washable cotton dress fabric, it can be laundered easily should it start to become a bit grubby.

This curtain treatment is ideal if you are short of time and money as it really does offer style on a shoestring. No sewing at all is required if you cut the hems with pinking shears to stop them from fraying and tuck in the top end securely over a wooden curtain pole.

The fabric used here has exactly the right colour combinations of turquoise and yellow and, being a check, adds contemporary chic to enliven all the other period details.

Take time choosing fabrics, and try out the alternatives on your sample board before you buy. Look at the remnants section in your local department store if you do not need large lengths.

DRIFTWOOD FRAMES

The framed picture above the toilet is an accessory that you can easily make at home. The driftwood frame is the important part. The driftwood forming this frame was collected on a beach — it is amazing how much there is in the flotsam and jetsam.

Look for four lengths of roughly equal size and width. Leave the wood to dry out thoroughly, then measure it into four equal lengths and cut it with a hacksaw. Assemble into a frame and stick together firmly using a glue gun.

To enhance the driftwood's natural roughness, rub some liming wax over the wood and buff with a soft cloth. The white liming wax will collect in the crevices, creating a weathered, sun-bleached effect. Add a picture by sticking it to the frame itself, from behind.

If your windowsills are too narrow to hold plant pots, use a slim glass vase filled with flowers to bring colour to your bathroom.

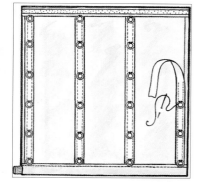
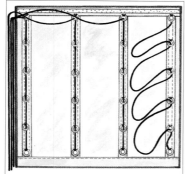
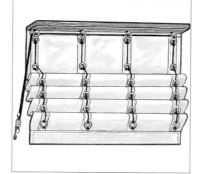

STEP 3

Using dressmaker's chalk, mark lines where the tapes will go, from the top of the blind to the bottom batten, 2 cm (¾ in) in from each side and at intervals of 30 cm (12 in) across. Adjust the lines for even spacing. Machine stitch the tapes in position, turning under the ends at the top and bottom of each line. Sew on the rings at 15 cm (6 in) intervals, starting just above the bottom batten and ensuring that they line up exactly.

STEP 4

Fix a narrow wooden shelf above the window and insert screw eyes on the underside above each line of tape. Stick the other side of the touch-and-close tape to the shelf and fix a cleat to the wall beside the window. Tie a length of cord to the bottom ring on the side opposite the cleat, and thread it through every ring on that tape. Pass it along the top of the blind and down the side to reach the cleat. Repeat with each tape.

STEP 5

Attach the blind with touch-and-close tape. Thread the first cord through every screw eye, the second through every screw eye except the first, and so on. Trim the cords, knot and secure to the cleat. Slide a batten into the bottom hem.

53

CITY SLICK BATHROOM

*T*he inspiration for this bathroom comes from the bright, multi-coloured fabric used on the chair cover. The design combines rich, primary colours in green, red, blue and yellow, together with striking black and white. The pattern is geometric and modern, yet combines classic stripes, diagonals and even trellis designs. Elsewhere the room is very much a monochromatic scheme in black, white and cream – only the accessories add colour. There is a practical reason for this: it is a quick and easy job to re-cover the chair and replace accessories for a new look, while the fundamental, expensive ingredients of the room are classic in style and design. They will not date and will also suit any subsequent decorative treatments.

This bathroom is an interesting combination of period and modern. The high-backed, elegant chair has a classical Greek laurel-wreath detail, yet the seat cover is twentieth-century modern; the walls have been painted to resemble ancient marble and granite but are tiled on the lower half with practical, factory-made white tiles. The bathroom suite has the square, moulded edges that call to mind the Edwardian period, while the mirror and cabinets are functional and unadorned, typical of 1990s style. It is interesting that, given this pot-pourri of colour and designs, the scheme still works extremely well. In fact, it is a fine example of the successful mixing of period and modern styles to create a truly classic decorative scheme.

SUITE CHOICE

As this bathroom illustrates, art deco or Edwardian-style designs can work well in a contemporary setting. Both are successful because they include square shapes and strong lines that enhance classic and even modern interiors. This is not so true of Victorian reproduction suites whose style is altogether more fussy, with rounded, decorative shapes and details.

By contrast, if you go for a completely 'modern' look and opt for space-age sleek designs, you will find that they inevitably date more quickly than the classic choice used in this bathroom. Once you have decided on the style of suite you want, buy the best quality you can afford. Personally, I still think that there is nothing better than a big, cast-iron bath – although 'plastic' baths have improved enormously over the years and some are now at the very top of the quality and price range. If you want an irregularly shaped bath or a jacuzzi, you may want to choose a top-of-the-range acrylic or fibreglass bath that are available moulded into a variety of shapes.

SELECTING TILES

Tiles are both expensive to buy and to fit. Here, standard, factory-made wall tiles have been used to good effect all around the room from floor to dado height, and to full height above the bath. Factory-made tiles are considerably cheaper than hand-made ones which are, in any case, too rustic-looking for this style of bathroom. In large areas, plain, basic tiles can look clean and smart, especially if they are white. Keep the grouting between the tiles sparkling clean by regular scrubbing with a toothbrush dipped in a weak solution of bleach. This is particularly important around the bath and shower area where hard water deposits quickly build up.

It looks unprofessional to leave the last layer of tiles just butting up against the paint or wallpaper above. Here some striking black and white border tiles have been added in a fun, harlequin design which mimics one of the geometric patterns of the chair cover fabric. Diamond border tiles really added

style to the sample board when placed next to the other elements being considered, and, although expensive, they complemented the plain white field tiles perfectly; lending them a more classy look. The final touch is a line of very thin black border tiles. These are particularly useful for finishing off the vertical edge of the white tiles around the shower screen where a line of harlequin border tiles would be too overpowering. Similarly, a line of the same thin black tiles has been laid at the base of each wall to finish off the last line of white tiles.

FLOORING CONSIDERATIONS

To continue the clean but elegant look of this bathroom, ceramic-tiled flooring has been used, which is both practical and smart. Reverting again to the classical theme, the idea of a plain white floor was rejected, and instead the black and white theme of the walls and chair cover has been reinforced. This white tiled floor with a black diamond inset tile offers the perfect solution: the floor is versatile enough to grace any colour changes made at a later date; it has a strong enough pattern to enliven the overall design, and fits well into the ambiguity of the period/modern setting. Fortunately, the design is so classic that it is readily available from tile shops in a variety of price brackets. Shop around for a good price, and try good tile warehouses as well as DIY superstores. If your room is not very big, you can sometimes pick up good discounts if you choose from their 'end of line' selections.

One word of caution: if you have young children or elderly relatives staying with you, ceramic tiles can be very slippery when wet, so make sure you always provide a bath mat with a non-slip rubber backing.

Another possible alternative that would have suited this scheme well is white marble. However, it is extremely expensive and also very heavy. If you do decide to use marble, check with a builder or the specialist who will be laying the marble that the floor will be able to bear the weight – you may be advised to have the floorboards reinforced.

STORAGE FIRST

Fitted bathroom cupboards are a great way to store towels, cosmetics, beauty products and dirty laundry, freeing up space and giving the room a very

This bathroom follows a mono-chromatic colour scheme combined with multi-coloured accessories and chair fabric. These can be changed with ease at a later date.

smart appearance. Free-standing furniture, such as wooden chests and cupboards, combined with open shelving look good in a country-style or cottage bathroom, but are just too cluttered for this chic, Italian-style bathroom.

Fitted wall cupboards and base units are now becoming as popular for bathrooms as they were ten years ago for kitchens. The best styles to choose are classic, white units which are wall hung. You can choose glass-fronted doors to display coloured bottles and expensive toiletries, but bear in mind that

these will also reveal less attractive items that you absentmindedly store away. If you are not the most organized of people, it is a good idea to go for solid doors or etched glass fronts. The doors used here offer a combination of plain base units with drawers for small cosmetic items, and a drop-door laundry bin (on the left). The overhead cabinets have a moulded, geometric-shaped cornice that mimics the square, Edwardian-style basin, and, when the cabinets are placed in a pair, they create a focal point that has a pleasing symmetry.

A clear glass shower screen fits in well with the clean, monochromatic lines of this scheme.

Tiles are fundamental to the practical nature and look of this chic bathroom. Remember to buy a few extra tiles so that you always have a couple of replacements in case of cracks.

There is a good range of fitted bathroom storage now on offer. Before you buy, get hold of a catalogue and compare it with the rest of your sample board to see how the style looks with the other elements in your bathroom scheme. Look out for small details: are the handles chrome or gold to match the taps? Does the style enhance that of the sanitaryware? If the units are wood, are they practical – will the surface become watermarked? Are the units self-assembly or will there be the cost of a fitter? Much the same questions apply as for kitchen furniture; so take your time. Good fitted bathroom furniture enhances not only the style but also the value of your home.

FAKE GRANITE BORDERS

In keeping with the classical influences of this scheme, the walls above the tiles have been treated with a fake marble paint effect. If you do not want to use paint – although this is by far the cheapest and most practical medium – look out for marble-effect wallpapers. These are now fairly readily available in a number of colours. Other effects are also available, including stippling, stonework and fake plaster. Collect together a number of possible samples and stick them to your sample board before you decide which to choose.

To add a smart detail to the 'marble' walls, try a granite-effect border. The simplest way to achieve this is to use a granite-effect wallpaper cut into strips. Buy a single roll, or even a remnant, if you can find one. Choose a fairly dark blue/grey colour that will stand out against the pale walls. First measure the drop from ceiling to tiles. Cut eight 2.5 cm (1 in) wide strips to this length;

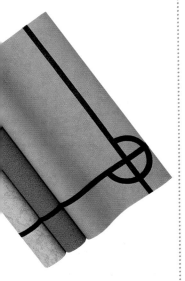

If you are short of time, rather than painting fake marble walls, choose a stone-effect wallpaper. This can be given a protective coating using a couple of coats of proprietary wallpaper glaze.

ℱAKE MARBLE

There is nothing quite as luxurious as marble-clad walls, but, apart from five-star luxury hotels and expensive bathroom showrooms, you hardly ever see it. Marble is not only expensive; it requires specialist fitting and expert advice to ensure that the whole lot does not come crashing to the floor. A cheaper, fun alternative, that looks stunning, is to paint your own marble look.

these will be used in pairs at each corner of the room and one either side of the bath alcove (if you have one). Using wallpaper paste, stick the strips in place, 7.5 cm (3 in) from each corner, starting at the ceiling and ending at the tiles. A plumb line may be useful for ensuring that the lines are straight.

For the top and bottom horizontal lines, measure across each wall and cut out 2.5 cm (1 in) strips to this length: you will need two per wall. Using wallpaper paste, stick the strips in place, 7.5 cm (3 in) up from the line of tiles and 7.5 cm (3 in) down from the ceiling. The vertical and horizontal strips should cross over at the corners. Finally, trace off and cut out a three-quarter circle of wallpaper 2.5 cm (1 in) wide, and use this as a decorative corner device by sticking it in place where the horizontal and vertical lines cross.

To complete the granite inlay effect, apply a protective layer of varnish. Give the walls three coats of acrylic varnish using a bristle brush, leaving each coat to dry thoroughly between applications.

TROPICAL TOUCHES

Accessories make a room special, and with bathrooms you have so much scope, choosing from a vast range of colours and textures. You can decant your shampoos, foam baths, oils and conditioners into attractive glass bottles, put coloured bath salts into jars and vases, and place them all out on display. As the colour in this bathroom comes mainly from the accessories, choose brightly coloured lotions and potions, and look out for tropical shades of sponges and towels in bright pinks, blues, reds, purples, oranges and greens.

STEP 1

Apply a base coat of cream, silk-finish emulsion. When dry, dip the tip of a feather into some dark grey silk-finish emulsion. Holding the feather loosely, run the edge of the tip across creating a pattern of veins. Some veins can overlap with others, but they should be in the same direction. Rotate the feather slightly as you drag it across the wall. This creates the desired thick and thin variations.

STEP 2

Before the veins have dried, mix a diluted paint solution of one part base coat emulsion to four parts water, in a paint tray and apply the solution to the wall using a roller. The paint should be transparent enough to allow the veins to show through. Smooth over the veins with a damp, clean cloth, using a circular motion, to soften any hard edges.

STEP 3

Using the feather again and some dark blue silk finish emulsion paint, highlight some of the existing veins. Vary the length and position of the highlighting — sometimes at the sides, beneath, or above. Leave to dry thoroughly. To seal the paint effect, apply two coats of satin-finish water-based acrylic varnish using a bristle brush.

Have fun making accessories — even toothbrushes — work for you while also adding colour to the bathroom scheme. Go for bright, acid colours to complement the modern designer look.

NATURAL CHOICE BATHROOM

*T*he inspiration for this elegant bathroom comes from all things natural: soft cream tones of textured cottons and linens in their virgin, undyed colours; rich, warm, textured wood for the floor and accessories, and parchment-coloured walls – all combined in a formula of simple, unadorned good taste.

You cannot really go wrong with this look – it is perfect for any style of house or interior, period or modern; its neutral colour scheme makes it perfect for an *en-suite* bathroom – whatever the colour scheme of the main bedroom.

When building up your sample board for this type of style, it is perhaps more important to think about textures rather than colours. Once you have your colour palette of cream, white and brown, it is more a question of mixing different materials than anything else. Notice how the shiny, white, porcelain handbasin contrasts beautifully with the dark grained wood. See how the paint effect on the walls gives them all the softness and texture of old parchment, and how the white towels have a deep pattern cut into the thick towelling.

This look is all about appreciating the quality, albeit in a very understated, stylish way – there is nothing showy about this look, but you will revel in the finished effect because it looks and feels so utterly luxurious.

Savons bois de
l'OCCI...

P1-80

P1-70

P1-5...

0020 - G50Y

0015 - G50Y

0010 - G50Y

HOW DO I LOVE THEE
SONG

PAINTED PARCHMENT WALLS

To set the scene, the walls of this room were painted with a delicious *café-au-lait* paint treatment to give them the age-old look of worn stone or parchment. This is achieved by a very informal paint effect using several different colours which are built up to create a more, or less, textured look, depending on your personal choice.

Start with pure white emulsion and paint the walls with one coat providing good, even coverage, particularly if you are painting over another colour. Then choose your first cream coloured vinyl matt emulsion. Look for a cream that sits at the extreme light end of the brown or terracotta family of colours on the paint chart. Avoid anything in the yellow section, however light it looks. Creams are deceptive colours to paint, in that, once painted over several walls in a room, they reinforce each other, so that what looked just 'off-white' on the chart can begin to take on a blue, green, yellow or pinky hue, depending on its composition. The only accurate way of knowing which tone the cream may start to take on is to locate its origin on the paint chart where it will be placed with its family of colours. Then use your sample board to try out and compare a variety of possible cream shades. Seeing them all together will highlight their differences. Having selected the right cream — probably the lightest paint choice on offer in the browns or terracottas section — dilute it with an equal quantity of water in a large plastic bucket. (For an average sized bathroom a half litre of paint diluted with a half litre of water should be enough.) Stir well with an old stick. The mixture will be quite runny, so make sure that you cover the floor and any other fixtures with dust sheets to protect them from splashes.

Take a clean cotton rag and run it under a cold tap, then squeeze out any excess water. Roll up your sleeves, put on rubber gloves and then dip the rag into the diluted paint solution. Starting at the top left corner of the first wall, begin to 'wash' the paint over the base colour, using large, circular movements to rub in the paint. Once you start to see the paint

being deposited on the wall in soft clouds of colour, keep moving across and down. When you take a break, make sure you are not leaving a harsh, straight line that is going to have to be repainted when you go back to work. The secret of the effect is to achieve soft billows of colour just like clouds, with no hard lines.

Once you have completed the room, let the paint dry thoroughly before you go back and have a look. If you want, you can leave it at that. Here, a second colour has been used; this time a mid-terracotta shade, built up with a few dense patches here and there, using the cloth dipped in a paint solution, diluted with four parts water, and using a gentle dabbing motion on the wall. The more layers of paint you apply, the more textured the effect. Use a progressively darker shade of the same colour in each case.

TWO-TONE TWIST

For a sophisticated twist to this bathroom, the fourth wall by the window has been painted using the palest pistachio green. To select a suitable colour to complement your scheme, try painting some samples on card and placing these on your sample board.

As before, the paint is not just painted flat onto the wall, but built up in watery layers to add texture. Start with a plain white vinyl matt emulsion base as elsewhere in the room, then wash over with the lightest cream colour as before. For the final coat, mix a paint solution of palest pistachio green, diluted with water and wash this over the walls. Only the faintest hint of colour is required.

This two-tone paint colour within a single room is somewhat reminiscent of the 1960s, when one wall would be painted in striking contrast to the others. But here the contrast is subtle and sophisticated, and uses colours of the same intensity. But it is also a great way to highlight a feature, for example the wall displaying an ornate fireplace, a fine picture or the area around a smart shower enclosure.

LEAVING ENOUGH SPACE

When planning a bathroom, or re-arranging your existing layout (perhaps to fit in a shower), there are certain guidelines to follow regarding space:

Natural colour schemes can be deceptive when it comes to choosing paint. Try combining a range of creams, beiges, terracottas and pale green shades to give the room a subtly textured look.

For a sophisticated twist to the colour scheme, one wall of this bathroom was painted pistachio green.

Place attractive sponges and brightly coloured glycerin soaps together and leave them out on display as accessories that are both decorative and practical.

- Allow at least 70 cm (28 in) beside and 1.10 m (44 in) in front of the hand basin.
- Do not position a shelf over the basin in such a way that someone could bang their head on it.
- Leave at least 1 m (3 ft 3 in) of space in front of the toilet.
- Allow at least 70 cm (28 in) beside the bath.
- If there is a separate shower cubicle, do not obstruct the entrance; if space is limited, choose a sliding door.
- Allow at least 70 cm (28 in) of space in front of the shower.

When you go to bathroom specialists or DIY stores, remember to pick up some free brochures. These will be not only packed with styling ideas that you can cut out and stick to your sample board for inspiration, but also planning advice.

Some brochures even provide a room grid with miniature cut-out sanitaryware drawn on paper, so that you can try out different potential layouts for your new bathroom. Stick a scaled-down layout of your bathroom onto your sample board and play around with different layout variations and with different colour possibilities for your scheme.

WINDOW FEATURE

The large floor-to-ceiling window in this bathroom is a beautiful feature – but, as ever in bathrooms, privacy could be a problem. The solution is to use the very finest white cotton muslin joined in two widths to create full, deep folds that are quite opaque from the street but still allow plenty of light to filter through. Voile and muslin do not need lining and can simply be double hemmed at the top and bottom and flung over a wooden curtain pole.

To achieve the regular folds, simply turn the muslin over at the top by 5 cm (2 in) and stitch a double hem. Feed fine, gold picture wire through the top of the curtain. By twisting the wire round a tiny brass cup hook at either end, stretch the wire taut as the cup hooks are screwed into both sides of the window frame. As there is so little weight in the muslin, the wire is quite sufficient to support the curtain.

To take down the curtain, just unscrew one of the cup hooks and slide the wire out. Put the curtain in a washing machine on a cold setting (to avoid shrinkage) with a bag of net curtain whitener. Once washed, shake it out and rehang while still slightly damp so that the creases drop out.

FURNITURE FOR LESS

This bathroom is a lesson in making the best use of space and employing storage solutions. The vanity unit supporting a generous size half-inset basin has a spacious cupboard beneath it which is the ideal hide-away for cleaning materials, floorcloths and other utilitarian items you do not want on display. Between the basin and the bath is the perfect storage unit: being tall but narrow it allows for plenty of storage without taking up valuable floor space, which is usually in short supply even in the grandest bathroom. Two drawers are good for smaller items, while the two cupboards in between are large enough to hold a week's supply of dirty laundry in one and clean towels in the other. This unit is beautifully made in solid yew, with a matching vanity unit and bath panel.

To create your own bathroom furniture, look out for a storage unit, perhaps to complement your existing vanity unit and then give them both the same paint treatment or fake wood effect.

Instead of reproducing a parchment effect in paint, consider using a similar-style wallpaper for the same look.

ℱAKING WOOD

If you love the look of this expensive dark yew wood furniture – but cannot afford the price, why not cheat and create the look of wood with a clever paint treatment? Try it out on card first and attach this to your sample board for reference. You can buy kits which will help you to create fake wood effects, or just follow these simple steps to give almost any surface the rich glow of wood grain.

Adding matching handles is a quick and effective way to create a smart, co-ordinating set. Give your bath panel the same look to complete the trio.

Do not forget to use your sample board to help you by collecting different pictures of bathroom furniture that you like. It does not matter if you cannot afford it – it is the inspiration that matters. Then search junk shops and second-hand furniture warehouses, and try to find a similar style piece or pieces that you could renovate, following the magazine cuttings for inspiration.

SECRET STORAGE

Smaller storage solutions are just as important and can go a long way towards improving the neatness and style of the most compact bathroom. Look for a small wooden crate or rustic basket and pile up fresh, white toilet rolls in it and place them beside the toilet. Use a simple cream, cotton string shopping bag, fill with sponges and loofahs and hang on a brass hook beside the bath.

For the bath itself, buy a smart, blonde wood bath rack, put it across your bath and fill it up with your flannels, loofah, soaps and brushes. Alternatively dig out a large wooden bowl or wicker laundry basket and fill with clean, neatly folded towels with a few new, white, perfumed soaps on top to give the towels a fresh scent. Another good device is a stack of hat boxes which can hide a multitude of sins from half-used hair conditioner bottles to last summer's sun lotion tubes and bath toys for the children. On a smaller scale a stack of wooden Shaker boxes will look decorative on the top of the cistern or on a little shelf and can be used to hide away cosmetic brushes and make-up.

ROMANTIC AIR

What could be more hedonistic than a scented bath by candlelight? You can buy a small wall-hung candlestick or go for a floor-standing candelabra: in either case, make sure you use non-drip candles to prevent accidents. Buy candlesticks that are in keeping with your decorative scheme. Here, there is a fleur-de-lys wall-hung candlestick as well as a wrought-iron, lyre-shaped candelabra, but all have white church candles and a curved shape as a linking theme.

Sweet-smelling scented candles add to the luxurious feel of this bathroom – but, remember, never leave lighted candles unattended.

STEP 1
Prepare the base by applying two coats of oil-based eggshell paint in a pale mustard yellow; the darker the wood you want to imitate, the darker the base you will need. Leave to dry thoroughly.

STEP 2
Take a small brush and paint over the surface to be wood grained using a mid to dark brown oil-based eggshell paint, mixed three parts paint with seven parts transparent oil glaze and two parts white spirit. You can buy the glaze pre-mixed in tins from art and craft shops.

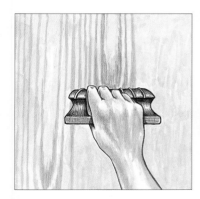

STEP 3
While the glaze is still wet, go over the surface with a graining tool, available from artist's shops. Drag it firmly across the wet glazed surface using a rocking motion. The grainer quickly creates the fake wood effect.

STEP 4
Stop the movement wherever you want to create a 'knot' effect. Work across the surface in strips. Do not lift the grainer until you have completed each strip. Leave to dry thoroughly. Apply two coats of varnish to seal.

PROVENÇAL STYLE KITCHEN

*T*he inspiration for this kitchen was a fabric table-cloth bought on holiday in southern France. The style is typically Provençal, in deep blue with a yellow paisley design; the central panel framed by an ornate border also features highlights of pale blue.

Such French-style fabrics are now readily available; other colour combinations include the primary colours red, blue and yellow, and you will also see emerald green, pink and orange. Provençal fabrics are an excellent starting point for kitchen schemes as they offer good guidelines for the use of bold colour combinations; they represent the essence of French style, which is easily continued with the use of care-fully chosen bistro-style china, glass and accessories.

As the starting point for the colour scheme, pieces of Provençal-style fabric in a variety of colour combinations were cut out and stuck to the sample board. Then a picture of an inspiring painted kitchen and samples of other decorative items were compared and contrasted with the fabrics, for colour and style, before the final selection was made.

CHOOSING A LAYOUT

This kitchen layout was designed around what kitchen planners call 'the work triangle'. This is the path that you take between the oven, sink and fridge as you move around and work in the kitchen. In a well-designed kitchen, this triangle should be fairly compact, to save you walking too far when preparing food. Also, and more importantly, the triangle should not be crossed by another pathway – say to the back door of the kitchen – or you risk possible collision, perhaps while holding a pan of hot water, or being knocked into by children running to the garden.

When you have decided on your final layout, draw a scaled plan of the kitchen, with the doors, windows, appliances and power points clearly marked. Using graph or squared paper for drawing up the plan makes scale calculations much easier. You can attach this plan to your sample board. It will help you decide on your choice of tiles, fabrics and accessories by showing which colours and styles will be near to one another.

Keep an eye out for pictures in magazines and take note of which layouts have been used, what combinations of appliances there are and any special design features that you particularly like. Then pin the pictures and cuttings to your sample board for later reference. Here, although the room is spacious, the work triangle is compact and positioned well over to one side of the kitchen, leaving the dining and sitting areas free.

CREATING A DINING AREA

If you want the kitchen to be dual-purpose, it is best to keep the 'working' part of the kitchen to one side. This will leave you sufficient space elsewhere for a dining table for entertaining guests and even, as here, a chair in one corner for relaxing. If the room has a natural dividing area – say an archway or a narrowing of the walls – use this to define your boundary. You can also help to separate the two areas with different lighting – perhaps overhead pendant lights in your dining area and low voltage halogen spotlights in the working part of the kitchen.

COLOUR SCHEMING

Having selected a fabric as the starting point, it is a question of translating the proportions of colour used in the fabric to the room itself. With this Provençal-style fabric, the base colour is bright cobalt blue, with secondary colours of yellow, pale blue and white. Obviously, bright cobalt for the walls is not a practical option; the colour is simply too dark and overpowering for the walls. The other alternatives are the yellow, white or pale blue used in the fabric, all of which would work as background wall colours. However, white can be too clinical for a large expanse of wall such as here – and pale blue is also a very cool colour which would not warm the north-facing aspect of this room. So that leaves yellow: a sunny, uplifting colour that is perfect for grey, early mornings; it is also a warming colour which will lift the cold north light that is a permanent feature of this kitchen.

With yellow being used as the background colour, white is a good choice for the kitchen units. It has a fresh, clean feel which is appropriate for a hygienic kitchen and, as you will see at any kitchen showroom, a wide range of different style kitchen units is available in white. Bright cobalt blue can be included effectively as the accent colour in the form of tiles – used here both in the fireplace and as splashbacks at the working end of the kitchen. The pale turquoise-blue can also be used as an accent colour, in the form of accessories and china.

PAINT CHOICE

Kitchens tend to suffer from more wear and tear than other rooms in the form of condensation and the dirt and grease that are deposited during cooking. A practical choice of paint for kitchen walls is therefore oil-based eggshell, which can be wiped or washed down regularly, unlike ordinary water-based emulsions.

Another alternative is offered by the paint ranges that are specially formulated for kitchens and bathrooms. These are manufactured to be moisture-resistant and to withstand condensation better than emulsion paints; some also contain a fungicide to inhibit mould growth, but all are extra durable and can be washed to remove grease and dirt. Look out for ready-mixed ranges at your local paint or DIY

Use bold, primary colours for Provençal-style rooms. Here a combination of bright yellow, deep cobalt blue and touches of ochre and pale blue is used.

If possible, find room for a comfortable chair in your kitchen where you can put your feet up for a moment.

store. If possible, buy a small tester pot and try it out on your sample board before you buy. Ready-mixed, off-the-shelf paint ranges are slightly cheaper, but you will find that the colours available are often fairly insipid and certainly more limited in choice.

Even if you have the luxury of large rooms, it is usually a good idea to leave the ceilings pure white. The addition of a colour, albeit the same as that used on the walls, can often have a claustrophobic effect. In particular, designers rarely use colour on a kitchen ceiling because it can distort the appearance of food during preparation and cooking. A white ceiling will reflect a pure, true light.

THE RIGHT UNITS

There is now a variety of ways to buy kitchen units. You can go to a nationwide kitchen showroom, to a DIY superstore, to a specialist kitchen designer who may be pricey but who could give you some good tips and ideas, or you can get a kitchen expert or joiner to come to your home and build a kitchen to your exact requirements.

The kitchen units shown here were made to measure *in situ* by a carpenter and then painted. If you can find someone whose work is of good quality and you know exactly what you want, this can be a particularly good idea for small kitchens, the benefit

Search junk shops for china to complement your colour scheme. Better still, take a trip to France and come back with a few pieces of authentic rustic crockery.

75

being that a carpenter will make units to fit every available nook and cranny, so no space is wasted. You will also have an infinite choice – you can opt for a simple run of base and wall units or choose a built-in dresser with open shelving, as here. You can choose chicken-wire doors, glazed doors, solid doors or fretwork – the choice is really only limited by how good your carpenter is. Show him or her exactly what you have in mind, using your sample board and sketches to illustrate your ideas.

If you intend to paint the units, the best material to have them made up in is super-smooth MDF. Use an oil-based eggshell paint, or gloss for a shiny finish. Choose unusual handles for your cupboards if you are not buying units from a standard kitchen range (or even if you are, although this will add to the cost). This makes for individual appeal – nobody else will have quite the same kitchen. Here, clear acrylic knobs that look like crystal were the best choice.

You do not have to stick slavishly to Provençal styling – the odd contrasting accessory can even help the look. Here, large checks provide a striking contrast to the Provençal theme.

FRENCH DRESSER

To reflect the French farmhouse kitchen feel in this room, the carpenter incorporated a dresser in the centre of one wall. Since the room is generously proportioned and the walls are spacious, the dresser could be large without becoming overpowering. In fact, although it looks like a freestanding unit, it is actually not a dresser at all. It consists of three open shelves over a run of base units (including the fridge) fitted in between the window frame and a natural alcove.

Above the work surface the open shelves provide a storage area for large items such as serving platters and tall vases, which are difficult to store in standard-sized kitchen units. When placed on shelves they create a very attractive display, giving the kitchen a distinctly French look. A neat row of cup hooks screwed into the bottom shelf provides the perfect place to display a decorative collection of tea cups.

ℐILING MADE EASY

Tiling is easier than you think, particularly if there are no awkward shapes and nooks or crannies to tile around. Tiling your own splashbacks or fireplace will save you a lot of money. Once you get the hang of it, you can even stagger the tiles, brick style.

STEP 1

If tiling over plastered walls, make good any loose plaster using a fine surface filler. Leave to dry and sand down to give a fine finish. Do not tile over plaster that is less than four weeks old and, in any case, it is advisable to paint the plaster with a plaster 'primer' before tiling. Using a spirit level, check that the work surface is perfectly straight before you start.

TILE STYLE

Deep blue tiles – the colour taken from the French style fabric – are a smart and practical choice for this kitchen. They contrast perfectly with the yellow walls and white units.

It is a good idea to link various areas of a room by one visual effect, and here the tiles have been considered in this way, also being used to line the inside of the fireplace on the other side of the room.

If strong enough, tiles can also be used as a work surface, for which you can buy a tile 'bed' with a light wood edging to finish off the look. The only disadvantage with tiled kitchen work surfaces is that you have to keep them meticulously clean with regular applications of bleach on a small scrubbing brush; apart from this, they are very practical.

A COSY CORNER

If you have the space, you might like to create a small seating area at one end of your kitchen.

Here, the corner between the second dresser and the fireplace is just big enough for a small, upholstered chair. The chair was a junk-shop find, but the shape was attractive and all the padding was intact. Blue and white check fabric was chosen to complement the nearby tiles and the same fabric was also used to make a roller blind above the sink on the working side of the room.

Choosing patterns such as checks or stripes to complement Provençal paisley fabric prevents the scheme from becoming too staid and predictable, and these fabrics also add designer flair. If you are not sure whether going off at a tangent like this will work, take a swatch of the possible fabric choice and pin it to the sample board. Live with it for a few days before deciding, perhaps placing it around the room. Usually, as long as you stick to the same palette of colours and the same style accessories, it can work very well. Beware, however, of trying to combine too many different patterns in one room.

Select possible tile designs and bring some individual samples home to compare with other swatches on your sample board. Only when you are absolutely sure, should you go ahead and make your purchase.

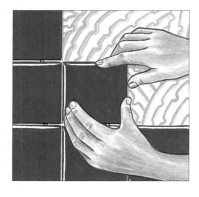

STEP 2

'Shuffle' the tiles well to ensure even mixing of any colour variations. Use a non-slip, water-resistant, white, ceramic wall tile adhesive. Using a spreader, apply a 3 mm (⅛ in) bed of adhesive to an area of wall 1.5 m (5 ft) square. Comb the adhesive with a notched spreader to leave a ribbed surface.

STEP 3

Place the first tile in the corner and push it home firmly with a slight twisting action. Place the next tile adjacent to the first, allowing space for the grout joint. Some machine-made tiles feature built-in spacer 'lugs', but with most you will have to use tile 'spacers'. Continue to tile, placing the tiles sideways and upwards.

STEP 4

If you need to cut your tiles, most machine-made wall tiles can be cut with a hand-held cutter. Mark the glazed tile surface where it needs to be cut, score down the line with a tungsten carbide wheel and use the jaws of the cutter to create a clean break. Curves and more complex shapes can be gradually 'nibbled away' with a pair of tile pincers.

STEP 5

The tiles should be left for 12–24 hours to bed firmly before grouting. Apply the grout with a rubber squeezee or grouting trowel, working back and forth across the tiles until all the joints are completely filled. As the grout dries, wipe away any smears.

COUNTRY STYLE KITCHEN

*T*he decorative basis for this kitchen is a light, airy scheme with cream painted units, cream walls and a light stone floor. As this kitchen is a small galley, a pale, uniform colour treatment was chosen to give it a more spacious and streamlined look. The house itself is Victorian, so a period-style kitchen was deemed to be a good choice. The finished scheme is therefore a compromise between creating a feeling of space and adding rustic Victorian charm, but without the usual dark wood and terracotta flooring materials which would overwhelm such a small kitchen.

The look is simple yet cheerful, with colour added in the form of country-style accessories in green and hot orange tones, including terracotta pots, wicker bowls and earthenware china with cockerel motifs. The style of the kitchen cupboards was, to a certain extent, already determined, as, for reasons of cost, the good quality units were retained and simply updated with a paint treatment rather than being ripped out and replaced in a complete renovation.

If your kitchen is practical but you want an updated look, think about having just the door fronts replaced – or repainted – to give the room a completely new look. This will cost a fraction of the price that starting from scratch can involve and is an increasingly popular choice. You can repaint over melamine, wood, MDF or existing painted surfaces.

NEW LOOKS FOR UNITS

The cupboard doors, which are of good quality, had been stained to resemble red mahogany. The effect was far too heavy for the small kitchen, which needed a much lighter look.

Cream is a good colour choice; like white, it is clean-looking, light and reveals grime and dirt so it is also a hygienic choice. But, unlike white, cream will not look too clinical and cold, so it is a good choice for a modern, country-style kitchen such as this. Play around with different paint colours on your sample board – see which shades enhance your chosen curtain fabric, your china, tiles and flooring samples. Kitchens contain so many standard fixtures that it is important, when you do get the choice, to select exactly the best shade for your scheme.

Once you have selected your paint, prepare the surface for painting. If you are painting over a very shiny surface, such as melamine, rub it down using sandpaper to create a 'key' to hold the paint. Even oil-based paint will not adhere properly to a shiny substance; it tends to chip off, so you need to rub down the surface with care. Skimping on preparation time now means that you will have to do the work again at a later date. It is far easier to sand down the doors once they have been removed as you can work better on a horizontal surface.

Once you have rubbed down all the doors, brush off any dust and wipe over each door with a lint-free cloth dampened with white spirit. Leave to dry. Then paint the doors with an oil-based undercoat. (As the old colour of these doors was a lot darker than the new paint colour being applied, two coats of the new colour were needed.) Finally, apply two top coats of oil-based paint. Rub down with very fine-grade sandpaper between coats; then dust off with a dry brush and wipe down with a cloth dampened with white spirit. While the final coat dries, rub down, prepare and paint the unit carcasses in the same way. Once dry, re-hang the doors on their hinges.

If you want to give the units a more rustic look, you can replace standard internal hinges with heavy, French-style, ornate brass hinges that are visible on the outside of the doors. It is also a good idea to replace the old door knobs with new ones to consolidate the change in style. Here, small, solid marble door knobs were used. Simply unscrew your existing unit handles and screw the new ones into the holes; most door knobs are made to fit a standard screw size so you should not have to do any drilling or filling.

GRANITE WORKTOPS

To enhance the stylish effect of the new-look units, here imitation granite worktops were used to replace the existing ones. This granite effect is highly realistic as it combines a photographic reproduction of real granite with a high-gloss protective finish that looks exactly like the real thing. The benefits are obvious: imitation granite is far cheaper and a lot lighter than the real thing. If you insist on buying real granite, consider it as an investment purchase. You will not be able to take it with you when you move, but it may add value to your home. If you intend to spend many years in your existing home, then it is an extremely durable and highly attractive natural material. Most real granite is sold by the fitted length as specialist equipment is needed to cut and fit it to your exact requirements. Make sure there are no hidden extras when you agree on the purchase.

If you go for the imitation version, remember that it is not as hard as real granite, so china will not smash should it fall on the work surface. However, it is also not as durable as real granite, so make sure that you always use a wooden chopping board when preparing food or you will start to notice tiny scratches in the high gloss surface.

PERFECT PELMETS

Kitchen windows require, above all else, a practical treatment and often this means roller blinds. What makes these unique is their spring mechanism, which means that, when the blind is rolled up the whole window is on view. When fully extended, the blind covers the whole window but still lets in some daylight, especially if it is a light-coloured fabric.

Apart from letting in maximum natural daylight, roller blinds can easily be kept clean by wiping with a lint-free cloth and there are no folds or crevices in

For a small kitchen, keep to a scheme that enhances natural light and gives a greater feeling of space. Here soft cream is combined with touches of green and terracotta.

With cream-painted doors and smart marble door knobs, these units look like a completely new kitchen.

which grease and grime can collect.

Perhaps the only disadvantage of roller blinds is that the mechanism can look a little utilitarian. To hide the roller, add an attractive pleated pelmet, which is very simple to make.

 Measure the width of your window and multiply this by one-and-a-half times to calculate the width of fabric needed. Measure the drop required: you will only need about 25–30 cm (10–12 in), depending on the size of the window, plus 2.5 cm (1 in) all round for turnings. Double hem the edges all round, then lay heading tape on the pelmet fabric, aligned with the top edge. Pin, tack and sew the tape in place. Gather the heading tape until the pelmet is the required width to fit the window. Fit the hooks and hang from a track positioned just above the roller-blind mechanism.

Here, unadorned cream roller blinds maintain the plain simplicity of the kitchen, while the pelmets add a touch of colour in rust *toile de Jouy* on a mustard background.

PAINTING OVER TILES

If you have inherited a tiled kitchen but do not like the design, a short-term alternative to having the tiles ripped out is to paint over them. If done properly, the effect should last until you can afford the tiles of your choice. Once again, preparation is the important thing, and should prevent the paint from flaking or chipping off the shiny, ceramic surface.

First, remove all traces of grease from the surface of the tiles. Do this using methylated spirits or

For a versatile, classic look choose plain tiles and units and then add colour in the form of decorative accessories and smart kitchen implements.

acetone absorbed onto a clean, lint-free cloth. These substances are flammable and toxic so wear a mask and gloves and work in a well-ventilated area. Wipe the cloth over the tiles to remove dirt and grease, and let the solvent evaporate naturally.

Paint over the tiled surface with a metal primer to help the paint adhere to the surface. When dry, paint over the primed tiles with two coats of cream, oil-based paint, using gloss for a shiny finish, or eggshell for a slight sheen. Alternatively, you can use ceramic spray paint, which is specially formulated to cover ceramic surfaces, but bear in mind that you will have to painstakingly mask off the rest of the kitchen to avoid the spray covering other surfaces.

If you want to give plain white ceramic tiles a designer look, paint on your design using ceramic paint and a fine artist's brush. There are several kinds of ceramic paint available; some are water-based, others are solvent-based. Some kinds have to be baked in an oven, so avoid this type. Most non-bake ceramic paints take at least 24 hours to cure thoroughly, so make sure that the tiles are left undisturbed while the paint dries. The non-bake paint should not come into contact with foodstuffs, even when dry.

SHELVING AND STORAGE

In a narrow galley kitchen such as this, special attention has to be paid to organizing storage and utilizing every available bit of space. If you find that standard units take up too much floor area, you could have your units custom made. A cheaper option is to look

Handmade Mexican tiles are just right for this style if you prefer coloured tiles. Look for designs that combine the colours in the rest of the room.

𝒮TENCILLING A BORDER

A simple, one-colour border can add a chic, designer finish to a plain kitchen. Cutting your own stencil design is more fun then buying one ready-made, and you can take inspiration from existing wallpaper, china or fabric designs.

STEP 1

Select the border you would like to copy, then trace the design onto tracing paper with a pencil. Turn the tracing paper over and place it on stencil card. Go over the reverse with a soft pencil to transfer the pattern onto the stencil card beneath. Carefully cut around the pattern using a sharp craft knife. Do not cut away too much card or the linking areas ('bridges') may be weak and tear.

out for the extra-narrow units that major kitchen unit manufacturers now produce; these are particularly useful for galley kitchens.

Other space-savers include corner units and midway shelving, which can help to transform even the most compact kitchen into a well-designed, functional room.

Here the microwave has been slotted in beneath the work surface, using an off-cut of the imitation granite work surface as shelving. Beneath it is a wine rack, while on top of the wall units, well out of the way, is a collection of wicker baskets, large dishes and serving pans. Decorative accessories can easily double as storage solutions so it is a good idea to consider the appearance of jars, pots and basketware when deciding what to buy for the kitchen.

Ceramic tiles are smart, practical and hygienic.

Make storage solutions as decorative as possible; store fruit in attractive baskets and put them on display.

  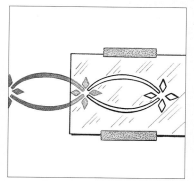

STEP 2

Make sure that your wall is clean and dry. Then, starting at one corner, place your stencil in position using masking tape or by spraying the reverse of the stencil with spray adhesive.

STEP 3

Dip your stencil brush into your chosen paint colour (use quick-drying acrylic paint). Then remove the excess paint by moving the brush briefly in a circular motion onto a piece of scrap paper; the most common mistake in stencilling is to use too much paint on your brush. Apply the paint to the stencil, using a circular dabbing motion to distribute the paint evenly onto the wall.

STEP 4

Once the paint is dry, which should be almost instantly if you use acrylic stencil paints, peel off the masking tape and lift off the stencil. Moving along the wall re-apply the stencil to the next part of the border. Apply paint to the stencil as before and move round the room until you have finished the border.

CARIBBEAN COLOUR KITCHEN

*T*his kitchen design was inspired by the china plates, with their bright Caribbean colours and pattern of tropical fish in shoals of pink, yellow and deep blue. Everyday china can be a good starting point for your kitchen colour scheme, as you can use it to complete the final setting, once the décor is finished.

The china selected here is perhaps rather a daunting choice if you are not confident in mixing and matching bright colours. However, once the colour combinations have been diluted, the only really powerful note of colour is that of the turquoise units, taken directly from the background colour of the plates. The other strong Caribbean colours of the palette have been used only as highlights and for accessories. It is important to note that the walls are fairly neutral, as are the wooden worktops, the floor, and the tiles, albeit with a black design.

If you are considering a strong colour scheme for your kitchen, lots of natural daylight will really help to lift the colours; poor illumination combined with strong colours can look rather gloomy.

PAINTING KITCHEN UNITS

As this kitchen is at the rear of a Victorian terraced family home, the scheme was designed in keeping with the period style of the house, but with an updated twist. The old units were removed and new MDF units installed which have panelled doors and tongue-and-groove detailing on the end units. A recessed wall unit with glazed doors was fitted between two high level units to create a dresser effect. Then, the look was dramatically updated with a turquoise paint treatment. Try different shades of paint on your sample board before deciding on the final shade. Use oil-based paints to produce a durable, waterproof coating; you can choose gloss for a high shine, eggshell for a semi-matt sheen or matt oil paint for a dead-flat finish. Oil-based paints take longer to dry than emulsion and you need to take more care in their application, so do not skimp on the primer or undercoat. Paint in a well-ventilated area as strong fumes are given off by oil-based paints.

For a professional surface finish, use a 7.5 cm (3 in) brush and, holding it like a pen, paint in three or four vertical parallel lines about 5 cm (2 in) apart, working over a 30 cm (12 in) square at a time. As the brush runs out of paint, quickly work across the vertical lines, from the top down, using horizontal strokes to cover the whole area with paint. When you have done this, use light, vertical strokes over the wet paint to finish. Continue immediately with the next 30 cm (12 in) square in the same way, working quickly to join the wet edges with a smooth blending of the paint.

Prepare the surface of the MDF by painting with a coat of primer or undercoat before painting with one coat of white oil-based eggshell. After the undercoat has dried, you may notice dust particles or even bristles embedded in the paintwork. Sand the surface lightly to remove these, then dust off using an old, dry paintbrush. Wipe down with a damp, lint-free cloth. Then apply the coat of white paint. When dry, apply the top coat of turquoise in the same way. To achieve the distressed effect, rub away the paint in places that would normally receive wear and tear, such as corners and edges. Use a fine grade of sandpaper and gently rub away at the top layers of paint, until you reveal the white paint beneath.

RAW PLASTER WALLS

Anyone who has been to Italy and seen the crumbling Tuscan frescoes will recognize the charm of rough plaster walls. They have a character and texture which complements many styles, looking equally at home with period settings or the exposed brickwork, chrome and marble of contemporary homes.

There are two ways to achieve a rough plaster effect: the first is to use real plasterwork, which must be sealed and varnished to be made practical; the second involves a fake plasterwork effect achieved using paint techniques.

In the first case, having walls replastered is expensive if it is just the look you are after, but if you are undergoing remedial damp-proofing, serious renovations, or removing wood chip wallpaper, you will probably be having the walls replastered anyway.

Leave the plasterwork until dry; this can take several weeks, during which large amounts of moisture will be given off. You may want to hire a dehumidifier to speed up the process. Once dry, apply a layer of plaster sealant and then two layers of EVA water-based varnish over the sealant. You can choose gloss, sheen or matt varnish depending on the look you want. Bear in mind that, once sealed and varnished, plaster is waterproof, but that, left in its natural state, it is totally porous.

To achieve the look of raw plaster using paint, start with two coats of palest pink emulsion, the colour of dry plaster pow-der. Then, using a lint-free cotton rag, wash over the walls from top to bottom, using a diluted mixture of one part pale pink/brown emulsion to four parts water. Choose a slightly darker shade and repeat the same process again, to produce the uneven colour effect of raw plaster. To find the authentic paint shades, compare your paint chart with a raw plaster wall to isolate the colour you will need to achieve the look. Play with the effects on your sample board first to decide which is most suitable.

Lots of natural daylight will help to lift strong colour combinations, such as that of the yellow, turquoise, blue, and pink shades used in this room.

Re-visit the fish theme of the brightly coloured china with a collection of hand-painted wooden fish. Keep them together in pretty shoals on top of your kitchen units or on the dresser.

This recessed wall unit containing a collection of china creates a smart dresser effect between two cupboards.

TILE IDEAS

Wall tiles provide a decorative and easy-to-clean surface. Tiles are particularly important above the hob, which is the area most prone to greasy splashes and cooking grime. The ones chosen here are 'encaustic' tiles. These are very durable and have a smooth, matt finish, which forms an attractive contrast to the plaster walls. Use a stone-coloured grout rather than ordinary white grout. Here, alternate tiles have a pat-terned design of stars or fish. These black motifs help to highlight the black wrought-iron unit handles and add definition to the working area of the kitchen.

NEW LOOKS FOR OLD CHAIRS

Instead of buying an expensive matching set of kitchen chairs, look in junk shops for wooden chairs with attractive but sturdy designs. Odd chairs that are no longer part of a set are often sold quite cheaply and can be a bargain if they are in good condition. To reproduce the look of these rustic chairs, choose something with a sturdy frame. If the chairs have already been painted, you will need to strip them back to the raw wood. You can take them along to a stripping tank, but bear in mind that the chemicals used are strong so the procedure may affect the quality of the wood, causing it to dry and crack. Alternatively, you can strip the chairs yourself using a proprietary stripper specially designed for

use on furniture. These chemicals are toxic, so do not inhale the fumes. Always use rubber gloves to protect your hands, and work in a well-ventilated area or outside if possible. Once the chairs have been stripped, wash off all residue of stripper using a weak solution of vinegar and water, then leave to dry.

To achieve a transparent paint finish, select a slightly darker shade of paint than that used on the units; try out some colour comparisons on your sample board first. Mix one part eggshell paint with five parts white spirit and, using a 2.5 cm (1 in) paintbrush, paint the chair, starting at the top and working your way down. Let the grain show through the thin layer of paint, using light, even strokes and following the grain of the wood. Apply a second coat if needed. Leave to dry. When you have finished the whole chair, use fine-grade sandpaper to distress the paintwork by sanding down the parts of the chair that would

Be adventurous! Select the colours for your room scheme from favourite pieces of china – the effect can be quite stunning.

A ROUND TABLECLOTH

naturally receive the most wear and tear, such as the slats, the edges, perhaps a raised knot or two, and the corners. Brush off any wood dust with an old, dry paintbrush and then wipe down the chair with a lint-free cloth dampened with white spirit.

To reinforce the distressed effect, take a 12 mm (½ in) paintbrush and dip the tip into the undiluted eggshell paint. With a light touch, brush over areas of the chair that are most protected from wear and tear: these include the horizontal supports at the edge of the seat and the centres of each back slat. You don't need to varnish the chairs – gradual wear will add to their faded charm.

IN THE SHADE

Good lighting is particularly important in a kitchen. Here, good natural daylight combines with under-unit lighting to illuminate the work surface and an overhead pendant in the dining area for evenings. The pendant shown here has been covered with a turquoise fabric shade. This gives off a soft, cool colour when the bulb is lit.

To make a fabric shade cover, take a standard white shade as your base. Measure round the circumference of the base, add 2.5 cm (1 in) for joining plus another 5 cm (2 in) for gathering. Then measure the height of the shade from the top to the base, add 10 cm (4 in) plus 5 cm (2 in) top and bottom for the elastic casings. Cut a strip of fabric to these dimensions and join the short ends together.

Turn over a double hem at the top and bottom of the fabric strip and form a casing. Into the top casing, insert a length of elastic that is just shorter than the circumference of the shade at the top; thread another length of elastic along the casing at the base – this length should be just shorter than the circumference of the shade at its base. Stitch the casings closed. Pull the fabric cover over the shade; the elastic will hold it in place.

Look out for tiles with unusual motifs to use as highlights within a plain tile scheme. Add them at random or use in a geometric arrangement.

Round tables are often the best shape for the corner of a kitchen as they make better use of a corner space than a rectangular table. A round table cloth made from plasticized, wipe-clean cloth is the practical choice for family breakfast or children's play time.

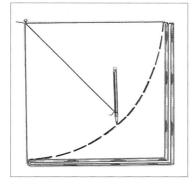

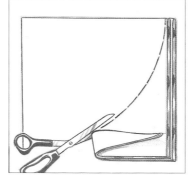

STEP 1

To establish how much fabric you will need, measure the diameter of your round table, plus the drop required. Cut out a square of fabric so that one side is equal to the diameter measurement plus twice the drop measurement.

STEP 2

Fold the square into quarters, right sides together. Attach a pencil to a length of string that is the same length as the quarter measurement. Pin the other end of the string to the folded corner with a drawing pin. Pull the string taut, and draw an arc across the folded fabric.

STEP 3

Keeping the fabric folded in quarters, cut along the pencil arc. If the fabric is too thick to cut through all four layers together, cut one layer at a time, using each previously cut layer as your guideline for the next layer.

TURKISH DINING ROOM

A summer holiday in Turkey and, more specifically, the rug that now hangs on the far wall, which was bought at a Turkish bazaar, provided the inspiration for this dining room.

The rug has a rich scheme of jewel colours: garnet reds, dark sapphire blues and touches of light golden cream. The design of the rug is equally dramatic with a central panel of diamonds surrounded by giant zigzags. Taking the shades as the starting point, the dark jewel colours were too overpowering to use on the walls of this fairly small dining room, yet to use the cream colour would have diluted the effect so much that the scheme would have lost that Turkish feel. As a compromise a deep topaz blue was used on the walls.

This was particularly appropriate as it was the colour used on the walls of the bazaar itself.

The topaz is the perfect foil for the colours of the rug, yet has a strength and depth of its own that enriches the whole scheme. The gold stars stamped on the walls give the room a magical quality of a midnight sky in the desert as they dance in the candlelight of evening dinner parties. As dining rooms are used less frequently than other rooms and very often at night or on special occasions, you can let your imagination run free and choose colours that you would not have in other rooms. Using darker colours is not a problem, as they are enhanced by lamplight and candles to create a wonderful, glittering party atmosphere.

A MIDNIGHT SKY

To reproduce the astral paint treatment shown on these walls, apply two coats of pale topaz blue emulsion paint and leave to dry thoroughly. Then, to create the uneven striations of darker colour, select a deeper shade of turquoise emulsion from the same colour chart as the base colour. Compare the shades on your sample board to check that they are compatible.

Dilute the turquoise emulsion paint one part paint to four parts water and, using a large flogging brush, apply the solution to the walls, starting at the top and drawing the paintbrush downwards to leave the paint deposited on the wall in rough, vertical lines, with the base coat showing through between the striations. You are not looking for neat, formal dragging here, but a more textured, informal paint effect. Leave to dry.

To further enhance the textured appearance of the treatment, take a lightly dampened 5 cm (2 in) decorating brush and dip the very tip into the undiluted darker turquoise emulsion. Then dip the tip into clean water and, starting at the top of the wall, draw the brush downwards to highlight the striated effect with more intense streaks of colour applied at random over the wall.

GOLDEN STARS

Once the walls have dried thoroughly, you can have fun applying a sky full of twinkling stars. The easiest way to do this is at random, using a stamp to transfer the paint onto the walls. You can buy a variety of stamp designs in the shops or send off to specialist mail-order companies for them. They also make mini paint rollers and supply a selection of paints in small pots.

Paint a scrap of card with the turquoise emulsion and leave to dry. Put some gold paint onto an old plate and gently roll the mini roller over it to pick up the paint evenly. Transfer the gold paint to the stamp by rolling over it several times. Once the stamp is loaded with colour, press it against the painted piece of card to test the effect. Remove it with one,

confident movement to avoid smudging. If you get an overly heavy imprint, you need less paint on the stamp. If you get a patchy effect but would prefer a solid image, try applying a thicker layer of paint.

Once you are satisfied with the effect, begin stamping the stars onto the walls. This is best done at random, unless you are prepared to measure out and mark a grid on your walls. If you are just positioning the stars by eye, do not stamp them too close together to start with, or you will be committed to a dense pattern of stars which could end up looking too busy.

If you would like to make your own stamp, use a square of linoleum (lino) and, freehand, draw a five-pointed star in the centre of it. Then, using a lino cutting tool (available from craft shops), cut away the lino around the design leaving the area of the star prominent. (Note that lino cuts more easily when slightly warm.) Test the stamp on your sample board before printing onto the walls.

CHIC SHUTTERS

Interior shutters have been used to screen windows since medieval times and long before glass became widely available. In hot countries they are still a common solution to the problem of screening out strong sunlight. In fact, wherever they are used, shutters lend a Continental look to a room and are quite unlike any other window treatment. Although they are expensive, shutters allow you to dispense with curtains, but remember that, as they are made to measure, you cannot take them with you if you move house.

A wide variety of shutter styles and sizes are available; some cover the entire window, others just the lower half, which is useful if you want privacy without cutting out all the light. The most sophisticated types have separate upper and lower sections that can be opened independently of each other. Most Continental shutters are louvred to control the amount of light entering the room, but remember that, when placed permanently across a window, shutters will dramatically darken the room, so look out for designs that can be folded back into the window recess as here.

Practical as well as chic, shutters serve to keep out cold draughts in winter and are a deterrent to

Rich, jewel-like colours define this scheme. Use emerald green, rich sapphire blue, amethyst and ruby red against a rich topaz backdrop decorated with gold stars.

Simple wooden shelves take on real designer style when edged with patterned fabric trimmed with zigzags.

The gold star theme creates the effect of dining under a desert night sky. The gold colour forms a striking contrast with the dark paint scheme.

burglars. Once fitted, they need only occasional dusting, or a coat of paint if you want a new look. Here, the turquoise paint used on the walls unites the shutters with the room scheme.

THE VERSATILE RUG

Rugs are highly versatile soft furnishings; they do not have to lie on the floor, although old kelims in rich, dark colours look wonderful, especially on wooden floors or over flagstones. Rugs can also be used as a heavy upholstery fabric, to cover a blanket box or footstool, or to make a tapestry-style cushion cover. Rugs and carpets have been used as table coverings

since the sixteenth century. You can follow this lead yourself and use a small kelim as an unusual table cloth. Strongly patterned rugs, such as flat-weave kelims, can also be hung from the walls to great effect and make a stunning backdrop to a Bohemian dining room. Wall-mounting is a particularly good idea if the rug is too valuable or delicate to use on the floor.

Choosing a rug can be a daunting task as there is such a vast choice of styles and prices. Prices depend, to a great extent, on the age and intricacy of the rug, as well as the size. Choose what appeals to you personally, something around which you would like to build up a colour scheme, for example. If you cannot find anything in your price bracket you could buy a reproduction rug. These modern rugs are still made using natural dyes and are often inspired by authentic, old Turkish or Middle Eastern designs. They need to become a little worn before they begin to take on the attractive patina of age.

When laying a rug on a polished wooden or stone floor, always use a recommended underlay or non-slip matting to prevent accidents.

SHELF EDGING

Open shelves create a useful device for the storage of china and wine glasses, which are often too attractive to hide away in cupboards and can be displayed in this way with little effort or expense.

Here six ornate, wrought-iron brackets, painted matt black, support a trio of plain wooden shelves.

The shelving takes on a special designer style when it is painted to blend with the walls and edged with fabric, perhaps cut into an interesting shape such as scallops or zigzags as here.

 To do this, measure the length of your shelves and cut a strip of fabric to the same length. The dark, ethnic-style fabric used here echoes the zigzag pattern of the kelim hanging on the wall. This is the beauty of using a sample board to refer back to – it prevents impulse purchases and costly mistakes, and allows you to select exactly the right materials to complement your room scheme.

Draw a diamond design onto the fabric or cut around the diamonds of a patterned fabric to create decorative zigzags. Use fabric glue to stick the fabric to the edge of the shelves. The edging not only adds a handsome detail but also gives the shelves a more

Coloured glass is perfect for this dining room. For an unusual and sophisticated effect, look out for heavy, emerald green goblets.

WALL HANGING

Transform the whole character of your dining room with an oriental carpet, dhurrie or richly coloured kelim used as a characterful wall hanging. Choose either a genuine or reproduction rug; all but the very largest can be hung easily using a carpet gripper rod, which has rows of sharp spikes to hold the rug in place securely.

solid appearance. You could just as easily use a wall-paper border or fringed trimming, but for this room a kelim-inspired fabric fits perfectly.

TURKISH-STYLE FURNITURE

The heavy, carved oak table and chairs are actually reproduction, Jacobean-style English furniture, yet they are the right weight and colour for a Turkish-style room. The sideboard is a useful piece, with drawers to store cutlery and table linen, while its surface provides a storage area for decanters of wine and platters of grapes or cheese.

You can find similar traditional oak furniture at antique and bric-à-brac shops at reasonable prices. Look for strong, solid pieces in dark wood with carved detailing. Alternatively, you could opt for heavy colonial-style furniture from India which would go well with this look.

CUSTOMIZING SEATING

Chairs make an important statement in any dining room. A good choice are those with removeable, drop-in seats. Take out the seat pads and re-cover them with kelim-style fabric or even old kelims themselves, if you can afford them. Staple the fabric to the reverse of the seat pad using an upholstery staple gun, mitring the corners neatly so that they are not too bulky to drop back in position.

To update plain, high-backed chairs, use loose covers that can be slipped over. Here, for instance, you could choose plain, gold-coloured silk and make floor-length covers tied on with gold cord.

Soft velvet cushions would give an exotic, harem look to this setting; choose deep, ruby red or sapphire blue to complement the rich, jewel-inspired colour scheme.

Candlelight is the only way to illuminate the table in this romantic dining room. Look for a gold candelabra and use scented candles for a heady atmosphere.

 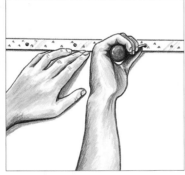 

STEP 1

Measure and cut a length of carpet gripper rod so that it is 12 mm (½ in) shorter then the width of rug you wish to hang. Remove the tacks from the rod.

STEP 2

Using a spirit level, mark a straight horizontal line on the wall where you want to hang the rug. Draw the line to the same length as the width of your rug.

STEP 3

Mark positions for screw holes on the gripper rod, about 15 cm (6 in) apart. Drill through the gripper rod; then drill corresponding holes in the line on the wall and insert wall plugs. Screw the rod securely to the wall, lining up the screw holes.

STEP 4

Attach the rug to the gripper rod, starting at one end and pressing the edge of the rug onto the spikes of the rod, so that the weave of the rug is firmly gripped. Keep the rug straight: you can reposition it if it starts to go awry. If the rug is fringed you may wish to conceal this by tucking the fringe neatly behind the rug at the top.

DUAL-PURPOSE LIVING ROOM

*T*his sitting room is typical of the knocked-through arrangement so common in many period-style family homes. When both a comfortable sitting area and also a formal dining area are required in the same room, the room scheme should be well planned, with both portions complementing each other in style and design. The sample board is the lynchpin in achieving this success.

The colours used here are the essential linking element. They were chosen carefully to suit the activities taking place in both areas of the room. The pink, green and white scheme is an unusual combination, yet one that works very well, as red is a warm, exciting colour, perfect for entertaining, while green is a relaxing, cool colour, good for quieter moments of reflection.

Stargazer lilies were actually the source of colour inspiration – their raspberry pink petals tinged with white and complemented by mint green leaves, presenting a fresh yet warm colour combination.

HOME AND HEARTH

The fireplace adds a feeling of character to this room, giving it a real focal point, but in fact, it is all an illusion. There is no chimney breast protruding into the room, and no alcoves on either side. Instead, the fire surround has been fabricated from MDF placed against the flat wall of the sitting area and screwed in place. To complete the illusion, the wall enclosed by the fire surround has been painted with matt black blackboard paint to resemble a chimney breast, but it has no flue or opening. This means that the fireplace is not functional but does provide a decorative focal point.

To copy this effect, take a large piece of paper and make a template, drawing out your preferred shape and style of fire surround. Look out for designs in magazines and keep cuttings of these for your sample board. Hold the template against the wall where you intend to place the fire surround, to gain an idea as to the scale required. If your room is fairly narrow, you will not want the fire surround to jut out too much, so bear in mind size and style as you work. A skilled carpenter will then be able to cut pieces of MDF to your requirements. If you prefer, consult the carpenter about design ideas before you start to choose the final shape.

Once the surround has been cut and assembled, fix it to the wall using brass L-shape plates, hidden on the inside of the surround. Paint the MDF with two coats of oil-based eggshell in either a contrasting colour if you want to make a real feature of it, or to match the wall. Here a subtle cream camellia colour is used on the main area and a raspberry pink highlights the elegant shape. To add highlights in this way, load a 12 mm (½ in), wedge-ended paintbrush with paint, wiping off any excess on a piece of scrap paper. Then, holding the edge of the brush steady, draw it freehand along the cut edge of the MDF painting a neat, defining line. Do this at the edge of the mantelpiece and also round the shaped, inside cut edge of the fire surround. If you find it difficult to achieve a clean, straight edge when doing

this freehand, and make a mistake, paint out the error and start again. You may find it easier to mask off the area using masking tape before painting the edges with the highlight colour. Carefully remove the masking tape once the paint is dry; do not leave it in place any longer than you need to or it may deposit a sticky residue.

You can use the mantel shelf to display accessories, vases or a collection of china. The space created by the fire surround is the perfect place to display a large vase of the tall pink and white Stargazer lilies that inspired the colour scheme.

CURTAIN IDEA

If you are trying to link two areas of one room with the same colour scheme, always use the same curtain fabric in the two different areas as it makes a particularly strong unifying statement. The window treatment you choose has a very powerful effect on the character of a room, so consider carefully the mood you wish to convey. Try out some sketches on your sample board or collect some magazine pictures of different examples.

Here, the versatile curtain design is at the same time both grand and yet contemporary; grand because the curtains are floor length and have a draped swag effect, and contemporary because the fabric chosen is a graphic check rather than a more traditional floral pattern. This treatment has several other benefits as well as its versatility, the main one being that you can easily make these curtains yourself, with little sewing skill. They are made from one length of fabric that is double hemmed at the top and bottom and at both sides but is not joined together or lined in any way; you do not even need to sew on curtain tapes. If using this type of unlined window treatment, remember to choose a reversible fabric. This woven, check fabric, which looks identical from both sides, is perfect. The way in which the fabric is hung over the large wooden pole above the window frame creates the elegant, draped effect.

The second advantage of this design is that if you move to another house, you can take the curtains with you and they will fit virtually any size or shape of window, with minimal effort. You just need to put up your pole and re-hang the drape.

Pinky reds, greens and creams make an unusual colour combination. Stargazer lilies were the source of inspiration and a vase of them in the room ties the whole scheme together.

The curtain treatment makes a grand statement – yet the effect is very easy to achieve.

Baskets provide a useful and decorative container for news-papers, magazines, cut flowers and fabric remnants. Look for old ones in junk shops and markets.

The only disadvantage with these curtains is that they cannot be drawn. So if you are overlooked by neighbours and want privacy, add a plain cream roller blind, set into the recess of the window frame. Roller blinds are cheap to buy and are readily available. To add a customized designer detail, make two long ties from your curtain fabric and either hand-stitch in place or glue these to the front of the roller blind in two evenly spaced decorative lines.

ALCOVE UNITS

Most people feel that they need more storage space in their homes, and a sitting–dining room is where you can really maximize on such valuable space. Generally the largest room or open-area in the house, the reception area has more wall and floor space and therefore a greater capacity for storage. If you incorporate smart storage features, not only will you gain valuable space but you can also enhance the look of the room – and even add value to your home.

One of the most common ways to utilize dead space in the reception room, particularly in an older property, is to build in alcove units. Where you have a chimney breast, the two recesses on either side are the perfect place for creating floor-to-ceiling storage. If the alcove units are made by a skilled cabinet maker, they will enhance the elegance of the room and highlight the fireplace as a focal point.

The most common design for such alcove units is a double-door cabinet to waist height topped with shelves up to the ceiling. This type of cabinet is the perfect hiding place for a video recorder, cassette tapes, CDs and video tapes, and the flat surface on top provides the ideal place for a television. Holes drilled into the unit mean that ugly electrical wiring can be hidden away, out of sight.

On the shelves above there is plenty of room for books, perhaps a table lamp or even a collection of glass and china accessories. If you intend to load the shelves with heavy books, remember to make sure that they are supported across their full width and not just at either end, or they will soon start to bow. If you are going to display glass and china, you might like to use glass shelves and fit low voltage downlighters or small spotlights into the top of the unit to illuminate your collection.

In this room the shelf unit is, in fact, a freestanding piece of furniture rather than being set into an alcove, but the effect is exactly the same. Note how the pediment at the top of the unit, the grooved side detailing and the painted panelled doors give the piece a decorative grandeur that lends style and definition to the whole room. The same idea could be repeated in the dining area where the storage

space would be perfect for china and glasses, table linen and cutlery. This type of freestanding, made-to-measure furniture creates an ideal linking device to connect the two parts of the room. Look for similar furniture ideas in books and magazines, cut them out and attach them to your sample board for inspiration and to refer to at a later date.

The other freestanding storage unit is in the dining area: an eight-cubicle shelf unit providing excellent decorative display space for glass, china and accessories.

Creating a unit like this can be fairly economical. Search second-hand furniture outlets and junk shops for freestanding open-shelf units.

To make the cubicles, cut and insert rectangles of  6–12 mm (¼–½ in) thick MDF and glue them in place as vertical struts, using wood glue or a glue gun. A good timber merchant or DIY store will cut the MDF to size for you.

Paint the unit with two coats of oil-based eggshell so that it links in with the colour scheme of the room. Make sure that you choose exactly the right shade of paint. Use your sample board to help

Lighting is very important in a dual purpose room as it helps to define the two areas. Choose over-head wrought-iron candelabra for the dining toom and elegant lamps for the sitting area.

𝒟 ECORATIVE CHAIRS

Blend the dining and sitting areas by incorporating the same colour scheme throughout. Make the chairs part of the scheme with a lick of paint and pretty, tie-on seat pads.

with this, painting brush strokes of possible colour choices next to your chosen fabric samples to ensure that you select the best shade possible.

To further incorporate the shelf unit into the scheme you could cut decorative fabric strips and glue these to the edges of the cubicle, or line each cubicle with a co-ordinating wallpaper or fabric, fixed in place with wallpaper paste or fabric glue.

ADDING A WINDOW SEAT

If you have deep window sills they are the perfect place to create extra seating in a small room. In this compact sitting-dining room, they are an excellent space-saving idea as the dining table takes up room where an armchair might have been placed, so the sitting room area is rather short of places to sit.

If you do not have deep sills, you can still incorporate this idea into your scheme by getting a carpenter to build a window seat for you. If you are going to the trouble of having this done, why not ask to have removable fronts or doors put on the window seat; this means that you can gain access to the area under the seat, which is a great storage place for hiding away board games, tennis racquets, table linen and spare soft furnishings.

Place a rectangular cushion on top of the window seat to invite people to relax and sit comfortably. An upholstery company will cut a piece of foam to measure for you, or you can buy a feather-filled cushion made up to your exact specifications. Cover the foam or cushion, using fabric from another part of the room, again this is an opportunity to unify the two parts of the room.

FLORAL TOUCHES

As the colours for this room were inspired by the Stargazer lily, it seemed appropriate to return to the floral theme for the accessories and finishing touches in the room. Flowers make a welcome display in a room designed for entertaining. Here, one flower arrangement comprises four tiny glass vases lined up along the mantelpiece, each holding a delicate white posy, while a generous display of Stargazer lilies brightens the hearth itself. On the dining table is a handful of tulips, brightening up the room and waiting to welcome dinner guests.

A few small cushions are a useful way to make window seats extra comfortable. Make some yourself with remnants from your curtain fabric or choose from the range of ready-mades in the shops.

STEP I

Take a soft, clean cloth, dampened with methylated spirits, and wipe each chair to remove dirt. Paint the chairs with two coats of soft white or cream oil-based eggshell, leaving the paint to dry thoroughly between coats.

STEP 2

Take a small quantity of a contrasting colour oil-based eggshell paint and, using a 12 mm (½ in) paintbrush, paint various parts of the chair to highlight the design – eg. the top horizontal back strut, alternate back spokes or decorative bands around the legs and cross bars. Apply a second coat for good coverage.

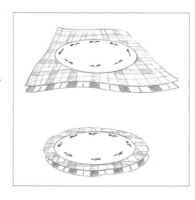

STEP 3

Cut a piece of 2.5 cm (1 in) thick upholstery foam to the same size and shape as the chair seat. Cut two pieces of fabric to the same dimensions as the seat, allowing 2.5 cm (1½ in) for the foam plus another 12 mm (½ in) all round for turnings.

STEP 4

Place the two fabric pieces right sides together, and sew, leaving a 7.5 cm (3 in) gap. Turn the cover through this gap and insert the foam pad. Handstitch the gap. Add four ties made from matching fabric or co-ordinating ribbon and tie the seat cushions in place.

GARDEN SITTING ROOM

*F*or this scheme the inspiration comes from nature, from the fresh greens of spring that make such a welcome appearance after a drab, colourless winter. If this fresh, simple décor appeals, look out for particularly pleasing tones and shades in this colour range. One of the best places to find such successful combinations of colour is in the garden itself. You will see some striking combinations that would adapt well as a room scheme: lemon and apple green, magnolia and mint, lilac and leaf green.

You may be inspired by a fabric that you have seen, in which case you could select one of the colours from this. If so, always take a piece of fabric to the paint shop with you as it is very difficult to carry an exact shade in your head.

A cheap and easy way to give your sitting room a make-over is by using paint. Here both the walls and floor have been treated to some stunning – yet simple – paint effects, including stripes, checks and stencilling; the finished look is highly original. Paint is such a versatile medium that you can use it to create many different effects. With a little confidence, paint effects are easy to achieve, and also easy to replace by simply brushing over again – much cheaper and easier to use than wallpapers, for instance.

CHOOSING YOUR COLOURS

Having decided on the clean greens of spring, the first thing to do is select the paint colours. Green is a good shade to use for decorating – it is fresh and clean-looking and will lighten and brighten the drabbest interior. It is also a good colour for both contemporary or more traditional interiors, representing harmony and balance. Think of pea green, lettuce and lime greens for a more modern interior, and soft peppermints, jades and celadon greens for a more period feel. For the scheme shown here touches of mauve have been added to soften the sharper shades of green, but still using the tones of nature – such as pale lilac and violet – for inspiration.

WAYS WITH WALLS

For this scheme two different paint effects have been used on the walls: a soft, dragged effect above the dado rail and broad cream and green stripes below. To create the dragged paint effect above the dado, and give the walls an ethereal haze, apply a coat of bright green emulsion paint and allow to dry. Then drag over this with a diluted mixture of one part paint to four parts water, this time using a slightly darker shade of green. Use an old paintbrush to achieve the subtly striated effect. Repeat the dragged effect with two or three more, similarly toned greens, leaving each coat to dry thoroughly before painting over. Any hard edges are blurred to create a minty, fresh look and the build-up of different paint shades makes the walls glow with colour and light, giving a more contemporary, tex-tured finish than plain, flat emulsion.

DADO RAILS

A dado rail is useful for breaking up two different paint effects on a wall – the dragged green and the green and cream stripes here, for instance. It is a way not just of creating character, but also of diluting a strong decorating effect that would be overpowering if applied over a whole wall. Look out for different alternatives to traditional mouldings. Most DIY shops now sell fine beadings for a more modern look or

Paint is a funda-mental feature of this room scheme, from the dragged walls and the cream and green stripes, to the checker-board floor and stencilled ivy trellis.

even MDF lengths that come ready cut into intricate shapes that are perfect for painting.

CHECKED FLOORS

A tiled floor looks wonderfully cool when it is hot outside, but it can be too cold and hard underfoot, especially in winter. In addition, ceramic tiles can be expensive to buy and fit. So, if you cannot decide between luxurious carpets or elegant tiles, here is a compromise that is cheaper than both: a wooden floor painted to look like giant tiles.

To transform your floors, pull up the old carpet and prepare the boards beneath by removing any old nails, filling any large gaps with wood filler and then sanding them smooth with an industrial sander (you can hire one of these for a weekend).

Once you have a clean, smooth surface, you can apply the first coat of cream paint. Always use oil-based eggshell paint for floors to obtain a practical, hardwearing finish. Leave the first coat of paint to dry, then apply a second coat of cream eggshell.

Use your second paint colour to create the tiled effect. Select the same green colour paint as that used for the striped walls, but this time in an oil-based finish. Mask off the floor into regular 30 cm (12 in) squares using a tape measure, soft pencil and low-tack masking tape. Once it is all marked up and masked off you can begin painting. Ensure that the room is well ventilated, then start in the furthest corner of the room and work your way backwards towards the door. When you have finished the first coat, close the door but leave the windows open to ventilate the room and assist drying. As with the background colour, you will have to repeat the process with a second coat to ensure a durable finish. When complete, give the floor at least three coats of matt oil-based varnish to provide coverage that will stand up to everyday wear and tear.

CHOOSING A SOFA

The key to the garden-style look is simplicity, so if you are incorporating patterns on the walls and/or floor, use plain materials elsewhere. Do not be put off the idea of a plain, cream sofa because you think it will be impractical. There are several alternatives available. First, you can ensure that the fabric has been stainproofed before you buy it (it will shrug off spills better), or an authorized agent can come to your home to treat the sofa with a stainproofing chemical that is applied directly to the fabric by hand. Finally, there is the choice of fabrics and styles available – look out for sofas with loose covers that are designed to be removed and washed in the washing machine. They are designed to come out looking as good as new, but without shrinking or losing their shape. Some companies even offer a free set of loose covers to put on the sofa while you are laundering the first set. Investigate what the large sofa and sofa-bed high street outlets have to offer.

If you do decide to invest in a new sofa, you will find that quality costs money; nevertheless, it pays to shop around. A good time to buy is in the sales when you can get some genuine bargains. If you have a small or awkwardly shaped room, another option is to get a sofa made to measure. This is not as expensive as it sounds, as many small companies who offer this service sell direct to the public, so cutting down on overheads.

SOFA THROWS

Not everyone can afford a new cream sofa to lend the coolness of summer to a room, but there are several ways to disguise your existing seating. Look out for the generous, French-style wraps now on the market; these can be draped and knotted over furni-

Paint colours will often look darker in the can than on the paint chart – the volume of paint may make the colour shade appear more intense than it really is.

Train real ivy over a painted trellis and then stencil more tendrils all around.

ture in a variety of ways. Alternatively, join together two pieces of fabric to make a large square, then sew plain ribbon or decorative furnishing trimming all round the edges to obtain an attractive fringed effect. Easier still, try using a simple square of hemmed floral fabric tucked over the back and under the seat of your sofa to add a touch of colour to link in with the walls and accessories.

FURNITURE FILE

To find furniture that is in keeping with this green scheme, look for metal furniture designs. The style is reminiscent of traditional garden furniture with a slightly Indian, 'days of the Raj' feel to it. In fact much of this type of furniture is imported. Look out for metal frames with attractive free-form shapes and designs; these are often combined with rattan seats or table tops. Many examples are fairly reasonably priced because of their country of origin and the styles will suit both modern and traditional settings.

A dado rail is a useful device to separate two different paint effects on one wall. You could use MDF or even ivy design border tiles for this conservatory-style garden room.

FLOATY CURTAINS

This light, summer look calls for a casual, floaty curtain treatment. To achieve this, replace traditional, heavy curtains with fine, white voile. The best voile to use is 100 per cent pure white cotton; man-made materials are rather stiff and do not fall into soft swathes in the way that natural cotton does.

To calculate how much voile you need, measure the height and width of the window, add the two measurements together and multiply by two; you will only need one width of fabric. Hem the fabric at both cut ends and then drape it into a generous swag over the window using one of the range of available swagholders or 'omkrets' that you will find in most haberdashers or department stores. These are simple, wall-mounted brackets with special arms. Simply draw the fabric through the arms, bunching it into a puffy rosette at each side, while the rest of the fabric falls softly to the floor in gentle swathes.

$\mathcal{S}$TUNNING STRIPES

The combination of cream and green stripes will really enliven the look of your room. It is best to avoid having bold, broad stripes over the whole wall or even above the dado as this can be too strong an effect for all but the largest of rooms. Use a dado rail to conceal the join between the two paint effects at the point at which the dragged greens meet the stripes. To bring the whole look together, paint both the dado rail and the skirting boards with the same plain green as the stripes.

FLOWER ARRANGEMENT

Plenty of flowers are a must for this look; experiment with armfuls of garden greenery and simply shaped flowers, as these have a more sophisticated, contemporary look. Other favourites are grasses, delicate green-tipped twigs and flowers with a subtle hint of colour; avoid unnaturally bright, garish shades. Arrange your flowers in interestingly shaped vases – clear ones are a good choice as they reveal the brilliant green colours of stems through the glass, which is doubly effective.

STENCILLED IVY

However wonderful the colour of your walls, you might like to bring a little more of the garden inside and you can do this by stencilling a *trompe-l'oeil* plant trailing over one wall.

 Begin with a small piece of garden trellis – you can buy it in various sizes from most garden centres. Paint the trellis with emulsion paint in a colour that will stand out against your walls, but which is in keeping with your scheme. Here a moody violet colour was used. Leave to dry, then rub over it with a damp rag dipped in some dark grey emulsion to add a slightly distressed look. For small painting projects such as this one you need only a small tester pot of paint, available at DIY or paint stores. Alternatively, look out for small tubes of artist's acrylic paints at your local artist's supply shop. This paint is water-based so you can mix it with water and wash out your brushes easily, and it is quick-drying, which is very useful when stencilling as it helps prevent smudging.

Fix the painted trellis carefully to the wall and then use a flowing stencil of a wandering ivy to cover the area around the trellis with life-like fronds and tendrils. Finally, trail some real ivy over the trellis from a potted plant placed on a nearby table, and blend the real leaves and stems with the stencilled ones to create a stunning effect.

Potted home-grown herbs create the perfect foliage displays for this look. Group pots together on a table or a modern tray to create an attractive focal point.

STEP 1

Paint the wall with two coats of cream vinyl matt emulsion. Then measure out the stripes at the required intervals (these are at 12.5 cm [5 in] intervals) and mask these off using low-tack masking tape. The smaller the room, the narrower the stripes should be, to avoid the effect being too overpowering.

STEP 2

Using a good-quality 7.5 cm (3 in) decorator's paint brush, paint on the stripes using green vinyl matt emulsion in the same base colour as that used for the walls. Apply two coats to ensure even coverage. Always avoid using cheap brushes that are apt to shed their bristles onto the newly painted surface.

STEP 3

Once the second coat is dry, carefully peel off the masking tape. Do not leave the tape stuck to the walls any longer than necessary as it becomes increasingly difficult to remove and could leave a tacky residue.

NOTE

If you are painting stripes all around a large room, you could use a roller instead of a paint brush and masking tape. However, bear in mind that using a roller will give you a more informal effect – and you will need confidence and a steady hand to get it right. Using a plumb line, mark the wall with vertical pencil lines before you begin.

SWEDISH STYLE STUDY

*T*he inspiration for this sitting room is the understated, naïve style of Swedish eighteenth-century drawing room interiors and, more particularly, the work of the Swedish painter, Carl Larsson. He is famous for the series of pictures he painted of the interior of his home, Lilla Hyttnäs in Sundborn, Sweden, at the end of the last century.

Scandinavian or 'Gustavian' style, as it is sometimes called, has such a well-defined colour palette and limited range of fabric designs that it is very simple to achieve an authentic look. The colours used are pale grey–blue, combined with soft, pure red and, to a lesser extent, navy. The prints and patterns used are checks, ginghams and small, close-knit, sprigged florals. The style uses painted furniture with fine, elegant and decorative lines. This look is very delicate, calm and genteel. Start by collecting together magazine cuttings that illustrate this style, or buy some postcards of Carl Larsson's work to see the artist's interiors through his own eyes. Many fabric manufacturers have produced collections inspired by Scandinavian style, and specialist books on the history abound, so you should not be short of material for your sample board.

SETTING THE SCENE

Start by painting your room with a backdrop of light grey-blue emulsion. Think of the colour of the sky on an overcast day and you will not go far wrong. This look is very simple when it comes to the paintwork – there are no textured paint effects here, just a flat covering of paint, so use a roller to get even coverage. If you feel the grey-blue might look a bit dreary, if you have a north-facing room for example, you could use cream instead and add the traditional Swedish grey-blue colour in the form of accessories and fabric. Collect together a few paint samples and try them on your sample board, and even on the wall itself if you are still unsure. Scandinavian style has a charm all of its own, but it is quite a cold look, particularly with pale blue walls. If you want to warm up the look, be restrained when applying the grey-blue, and play up the creams and reds.

STAMP STYLE

To soften the effect of the cool walls, this room has a border of pretty red hearts at picture-rail height. This is a good device for effectively lowering the height of the ceiling. The lower the border of hearts, the cosier the room feels. Here the top of the window was low enough for the border, but if you have very high ceilings with windows to match, you can drop the border down to 30–60 cm (1–2 ft) below ceiling height.

To ensure a good straight line, take a long ruler and measure down from the ceiling at 15 cm (6 in) intervals, working your way right round the room, marking the wall with a soft pencil at every interval. Draw a faint 5 cm (2 in) line over each mark, using a spirit level to check that the horizontal line is level.

Use a stamp to print a heart over each line (or they can be stencilled if you wish). Rubber stamps are becoming increasingly popular for applying motifs to walls. Take a mini foam roller and roll it in a small quantity of red acrylic paint, then roll the roller over the surface of the rubber stamp. Try the stamp on your sample board first to check that you are happy

Conventional Gustavian colours include light grey–blue or cream for the walls, delicate blue highlights, and wall decorations painted in deep blue and soft red shades.

with it before using it on your walls. Then roller over the stamp again and press it firmly against the wall. Carefully release it to reveal the image. Re-load the stamp with paint each time. When stamping the heart motifs around the wall, be careful to line up the centre of the stamp over the pencil lines, and keep the rest of the stamp parallel with the horizontal line. By the time you have worked your way round the whole room the paint should be dry. (It will dry almost instantly if you use acrylic paint, but this usually means that you have to work quite quickly.) Lastly, go back with a soft, clean rubber and carefully erase any pencil marks left on the walls.

CHOOSING FURNITURE

The right furniture for this look is authentic Gustavian furniture. Original pieces can still be found but are extremely collectable and therefore out of the price range most of us can afford. However, there is a good selection of reproductions in the shops, many of which are true to the original eighteenth-century archive designs; but even these are expensive. To create your own Gustavian-style chairs and tables from junk shops or second-hand furniture warehouses, start by looking out for the right shapes. Chairs should have fine, elegant lines and prettily carved details. For dining chairs, look out for examples with drop-in seats which can be re-covered with check fabric, in keeping with the Swedish look.

For tables, look for round pedestal designs with a central stem that splits off into three legs. The ideal shape would be a gently curved pedestal with carved turnings just above the three legs. There are many variations on these Gustavian themes and your sample board is the best place to build up a collection of cuttings showing the various examples, including bookshelves, writing desks and armchairs with wooden frames. Once you have bought a few pieces of furniture that are the right shapes, painting them with pale cream or grey eggshell paint will quickly transform them into the right look.

First rub down the furniture with sandpaper, finishing with a fine-grade paper to get a super-smooth surface. Then wipe down with a soft cloth dampened with white spirit to remove any traces of grease or dust. For the paint

The combination of pale, painted furniture, gingham fabric and grey–blue walls epitomises the Scandinavian look.

you will need to buy an oil-based eggshell paint in either cream or very light grey. Eggshell dries to a slight sheen, which is the finish that you are aiming for. Apply the paint using a small, natural bristle brush; do not overload it or you will get lots of paint runs. Once the first coat is thoroughly dry (it is best to leave it to dry for 24 hours), rub down any uneven areas using fine-grade sandpaper. Wipe down again as before, then reapply a second coat of paint. You can repeat this treatment with all the items of furniture you have bought to create a set, or use an

alternative paint colour for a couple of individual pieces. Upholster or re-cover chairs with gingham or larger check design fabrics for an authentic effect.

WINDOW TREATMENT

This sitting room has a simple but elegant curtain treatment; one that is easy enough to make yourself. The basis of the treatment is a roller blind in a small blue and white check fabric with a dainty, red daisy inset. The fabric is pale enough to let in some sunlight, even when the blind is fully extended, and,

Create your own Scandinavian-style pictures using hand-painted frames in a soft red shade. Combine these with handpainted flower or heart motifs in pale blue, and complete with a length of check ribbon.

when retracted, reveals the whole window. The bottom edge of the blind is left unadorned, but this is more than compensated for by the decorative swag above, which creates a pelmet over the roller blind and has asymmetric 'tails' that hang down decoratively at either side.

To make the swag, measure the height and width of your window, and multiply this figure by one and a half. Cut two complementary fabrics to this length, using the fabrics at full width. This example combines a red-on-white striped fabric with floral wave motif for the lining and a red and blue check for the main fabric. Placing the two fabrics right sides together, pin, tack and machine stitch together along three and a half sides, leaving a 15 cm (6 in) gap at one end. Turn the fabrics right side out through this gap. Tuck in the gap seams and hand stitch the gap closed. To add a designer finish, stitch a length of white bobble fringing to both short ends. To hang the swag, loop the material over a wooden curtain pole fixed above the window. Gently pull the reverse side down from the centre of the pole so that the lining fabric creates a full central swag, while letting the 'tails' hang asymmetrically, long on one side and short on the other.

LIGHTING THE ROOM

Used properly, good lighting adds to the character of a room, highlighting certain features, changing the atmosphere and enhancing the mood from day into night. For this scheme overhead lighting could have cast unflattering shadows and made the room feel cold and unfriendly. Instead, in view of the fact that the room is painted with a naturally cool colour, individual lamps light the room. Work areas usually require more intense local light, so there is a stan-

Paint a lampstand with cream eggshell and add blue lines to highlight the elegant curves of the stand. Finish with a pleated gingham shade.

$\mathscr{P}$AINTED TEA TRAY

Paint and decorate a wooden tray with red heart motifs and Gustavian-inspired filigree design. It is the perfect accessory on which to serve your guests tea and cakes when they come round to admire your Scandinavian-style study.

dard lamp in the corner, focusing light onto the surface of the writing desk. The warm glow of sunlight is sufficient to shine through the window and brighten up the room by day, but by night lamplight is more conducive to a relaxing, evening mood.

The lamp on the pedestal table has a standard tungsten filament bulb that gives out a warm, diffused light, and the red in the check shade also serves to warm the colour of the light given out.

By contrast, the standard lamp has a no-nonsense shade that gives out a clean light, mainly over the work area. It can also be moved to provide a good level of ambient light in the rest of the room.

HEART MOTIFS

A set of napkins or place mats is a good way to use up fabric remnants and, if you can link the theme to your study décor, so much the better. Here the red

heart motif from the wall border has been carried through on a set of pale blue check napkins.

 To make the napkins, divide the fabric remnant into four equal rectangles, each about 20 cm (8 in) square. Turn under the raw edges and machine stitch double hems all round. Check fabrics are much quicker to cut and sew, since you can follow the straight lines of the design.

To decorate each napkin, draw out a heart about 4 × 4 cm (1½ × 1½ in) on a piece of card, then cut it out. Place this heart-shaped template in the corner of each napkin, and draw round it using a soft pencil or dressmaker's chalk.

Take a length of red embroidery thread and begin to fill in each heart using tiny cross-stitches. Keep the stitches as neat and regular as you can on the reverse side as well as on the front as both sides of the napkin will be visible when in use.

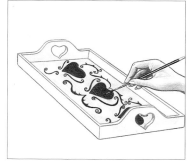

STEP 1

This method of decoration can be applied to any tray made of wood or MDF. First smooth down the surface of the tray by rubbing it with fine-grade sandpaper. Then wipe all over with a clean cotton cloth dampened with white spirit. Leave to dry.

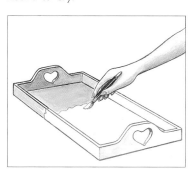

STEP 2

Paint the tray with two coats of pale blue oil-based eggshell. Leave to dry between coats.

STEP 3

Following the template (see above), outline three heart shapes in soft pencil along the length of the tray. Then fill in the hearts with red artist's oil paints using a fine paintbrush. Leave to dry thoroughly.

STEP 4

Paint over the swirls and tendrils linking the three hearts together with the red artist's oil paint and a fine brush. Finally, varnish the tray on both sides with two coats of varnish for a protective finish, leaving it to dry thoroughly between coats.

Heart motifs, particularly in a soft red colourway, are central to the decorative style of this scheme. Look out for suitable accessories in stores and antique shops.

EASY LIVING ROOM

*T*he curtains were the inspiration for this room scheme; brought from another house, where they had been used in a bedroom, they were the perfect length for the French windows of this sitting room. However, as the starting point for the sample board, the pink colour of the fabric was rather overwhelming. To tone it down, the other colours in the fabric, namely the cream and turquoise, have been emphasized, and these colours feature strongly in the decorative scheme of the room. As the room has well-proportioned French windows leading onto a sunny, south-facing garden, the curtains glow with a pink warmth during the day. To contrast with this, the deep turquoise colour used on the walls is both striking and modern, and shows just how well unusual colour combinations can work.

Elsewhere the room is fairly neutral in soft shades of stone which balance the strength of the walls. The choice of light, honey-coloured wood for the floor lifts the scheme even more, giving it a chic yet informal feel. Wood flooring serves to warm up all colour schemes, yet in a natural, understated way without actually adding another colour.

PLAYING WITH PATTERNS

In many ways this sitting room illustrates how effective it can be to combine patterns and textures for visual interest. The room is very simple in that no fussy florals are used, yet the *toile de Jouy* cushion, the soft, waffle throw and the elegant lines of the furniture add welcome softer touches. To start with the check curtain fabric leaves a number of options available for using patterns as checks go so well with many other pattern designs. Here, the spotted wallpaper pattern just manages to lift the turquoise walls which could have been too heavy as a relentless, dense block of colour. The sofa is plain, but, if you look more closely, you will see that the fabric has a damask weave to soften its strong lines. Try to balance out pattern, colour and mood in this way when you play around with the pieces on your sample board. See how making subtle changes will alter the character of your room; get it right and you will notice a real sense of harmony as the scheme begins to take shape.

FLOORING CONSIDERATIONS

Light wood flooring is a popular choice for today's easy-going, multi-functional rooms. If you knock through two small rooms to create one large living space, nothing is as effective in uniting the whole space than laying wooden flooring throughout. Wood has a natural charm that updates a room, yet in a way that remains in keeping with any style of home decoration.

Depending on what style or colour you use, wooden flooring will enhance any style of property: Victorian, Georgian or even a 1950s semi. It is also a practical choice as it is easy to keep clean and smart. If you choose a good-quality brand and have it professionally laid, it will stay looking good for years. However, take care not to lay wood flooring in an area where there is any damp – or the wood is liable to warp and bubble.

Many older properties have their original wooden floorboards hidden beneath fitted carpets. It is often worth revealing these, as, if they are in good condition, they can be sanded down and varnished. But bear in mind that they will never have the pristine look of the new wood shown here.

As hardwoods are a precious and slow-growing commodity, solid wood block flooring is very expensive. The shallow blocks, whose depth relates to the price you will pay, interlock to form solid panels or 'parquet'. Available in a vast range of different woods and stains, consider not just colour but grain pattern before you buy. Then lay onto a prepared solid floor surface and secure with strong wood adhesive. Unless you're very confident, it's best to have it fitted professionally.

Wood-strip flooring, such as that used here, is cheaper than solid blocks as the flooring consists of a veneer of the hardwood over a prepared base, often a softwood. The wood strip comes in random lengths which are laid parallel to each other using tongue-and-groove joints, to give the look of short, narrow floorboards.

Ask your stockists for a few samples to take home; try them *in situ* and against other elements of your sample board before you make your choice.

Leave the flooring to acclimatize in the room for a few days before fitting.

CURTAIN CALL

A simple, understated room like this does not need a grand, elaborate curtain treatment. Here, the thick, woven fabric itself is strong enough in colour to make a bold statement. The curtains are hung using 7.5 cm (3 in) wide pencil-pleat heading tape. This gives a good depth at the top of the curtains to balance the length. When calculating the width of fabric, you need to allow enough for two-and-a-half times the track length. When measuring the length, remember to add on the height of the pole above the window, plus turnings.

Wrought-iron curtain poles are stronger than wood and so are usually narrower in diameter. Use these poles together with wrought-iron rings to hang the curtains, and look out for attractive finials, such as the simple 'shepherd's crook' finial chosen here. Look out for different shapes and styles in catalogues and stick the pictures on your sample board. Remember to allow 10–15 cm (4–6 in) of pole to extend either side of the window frame to allow

This colour scheme is made up of a combination of pale pink, turquoise and cream. The turquoise gives the room a contemporary twist and prevents the pink from being too overpowering.

Unite other elements of the room with similar paint colours and fabric styles.

A staggered-level, freestanding candlestick made from cast iron will be an attractive feature by day and provide soft, flickering light in the evenings.

enough length for the finial to show up against the wall. It is best to line your sitting room curtains; this prevents them from fading in sunlight, increases insulation in the winter and helps the fabric to hang better. It is easiest to make loose-lined curtains, where the lining is attached at the top only. To do this, make up the lining to the size of the finished, ungathered curtain, turning in the sides and top and bottom hems twice, each time by 2.5 cm (1 in). Sew the top of the lining to the bottom of the heading tape.

SOFA STYLE

A sofa is an investment purchase; if you buy wisely and pay that bit extra for top quality you will acquire a piece of furniture that will last for years. If you buy a sofa with a strong, solid-wood frame, you can have it re-upholstered and re-covered many times. On each occasion the sofa will take on a new lease of life and, if you vary the fabrics, a new look. Choose plump, feather-filled cushions in preference to foam cushions which have a less luxurious quality.

After quality, one of the most frequent reasons a sofa is thrown out is the style. If you buy something that is very fashionable now, the chances are you will regret it in a few years' time. Far better to choose a design with classic lines and a timeless elegance; you can always choose a slightly more contemporary cover to liven it up. That having been said, one of the most enduring looks is a plain cream or stone-coloured sofa such as the one chosen here. Put it in any style room, whatever the colour scheme, and it will enhance the décor. Interior designers often choose plain, light sofas and combine them with armchairs covered in colourful checks or stripes that make an attractive style statement in small doses, but would be overpowering seen on a large, three-seater sofa. Remember that you can always add colour to a plain sofa in the form of cushions or a throw. Throws take various forms; a small blanket with fringed edging is perfect and such blankets are available in colourful checks or plains to enliven almost any

scheme. Alternatively, buy a length of finely woven fabric and, using a pin, unpick the sides until the fabric threads start to form an attractive, frayed edge. Once you have a 10 cm (4 in) fringe, machine a double row of stitches at the woven edge to stop it fraying further.

SIMPLE FRILLED CUSHION

One of the easiest and most versatile soft furnishings, square cushions offer elegant splashes of colour for chairs and sofas. Decorated with a frilled edge, cushions take on a designer quality, yet they are simple to make yourself.

 Start by cutting out two equal-size square fabric panels to the dimensions of the cushion you want, adding 2.5 cm (1 in) all round for turnings. To calculate the frill length, measure round all four sides of the cushion and double this figure, adding 2.5 cm (1 in) for turnings. Cut the frill strip to this length, neatly joining lengths

A contemporary-style sitting room will benefit from the look of neutral, honey-coloured wood-strip flooring. Other choices include sisal, seagrass or even stone flooring.

ℋOW TO VERDIGRIS

The most attractive paint finish for wrought-iron is 'verdigris' — the naturally occurring green, crumbly effect caused by corrosion of brass, copper and bronze.

STEP 1
Spray the surface with gold spray paint and leave to dry. Mix a solution of one part deep blue emulsion to four parts water and brush on this mixture.

STEP 2
Mix a verdigris paste of pale blue emulsion using two parts paint to one part methylated spirits, then sift in whiting powder to form a smooth paste.

if necessary, and remembering to add the turning allowance each time. The width of the strip should be double the width of the required frill. Fold the strip in half lengthways, wrong sides together, and press. Stitch a row of gathering stitches along the raw edge. Grasp the ends of the thread and pull the fabric up into a bunched frill. Spread out the gathers evenly and ensure that the frill is the correct length to go round the whole cushion exactly.

Pin and tack the frill around the edges of the wrong side of the front panel. Pin the panels right sides together, edges aligned, and stitch round three-and-a-half sides, sandwiching the frill in between. Turn the cover right side out and sew touch-and-close tape to the inside edge of the gap. Insert a cushion pad. Press the tape together to close.

WROUGHT-IRON FURNITURE

Furniture made from wrought-iron is perfect for this room as it has an informal style with open, softly

curving lines that pick up on the sweeping arms of the sofa and the wrought-iron curtain pole. Wrought-iron pieces are widely available and often well priced too. If you cannot afford the more expensive, designer pieces, look out for traditional wrought-iron garden furniture and update it with a verdigris paint effect, matt black paint or even gold spray paint, if you like a light, more baroque feel. You can also buy spray paints in a variety of metallic finishes such as copper, bronze, pewter and silver or even a textured, hammered finish.

Use your sample board to group pictures from magazines and brochures that illustrate how wrought-iron can be combined with other styles of furniture in room settings. You will see that it works well with cane and rattan, and also with glass in the form of small coffee tables. This sitting room has a stylish shelf unit that was, in fact, designed for use in a kitchen. It has a lightness of style that belies the strength of the metal.

STEP 5

When half-dry, take a clean, rough cloth and wipe off some of the protruding areas to reveal further layers of colour. When completely dry, apply two coats of matt polyurethane varnish to protect the surface.

NOTE

This technique is suitable for any metal surface. You can even use it on plastic to create the illusion of metal; the perfect make-over for cheap, plastic garden furniture.

STEP 3

Mix up a verdigris paste of pale mint green emulsion in the same way. Brush the two pastes over the surface together, to get a haphazard, two-tone colour. Vary the thickness and texture of the paste at random. While the pastes are drying, use the gold spray paint to spray over small, light patches of colour at random.

STEP 4

Dribble the surface with water to reveal the various layers of colour beneath. Then sprinkle some whiting powder over the still-damp surface, pressing it into the recesses of the metal with your fingers.

Creating a room with studied 'ease' and stylish informality is all about colour, shape and form. There's no space for clutter — keep a place for everything and everything in its place.

ONE-ROOM SPACE

*T*he red and cream colour scheme of this dual-purpose living room has such a simple clarity that it is difficult to go wrong with this combination. In fact, a subtle third colour is used here: it is not immediately obvious, but is important in uniting the starkly contrasting red and cream colours. The 'go-between' colour is a warm coffee tone which is used on the checker-board floor, the picture rail, the curtain fabric and the fire surround. It is a soft, neutral colour that warms the cream, yet does not compete with the red, making it the perfect partner to both.

A simple colour scheme is best enhanced by simple patterns. Here, stripes have been used on the day bed which is the focal point of the room. The only other pattern used is a single-motif design on the fabric of the cupboard doors, the roller blinds and the curtain edging.

The beauty of this colour scheme lies in the use of unbleached, natural fabrics and materials. Look out for calico, raw linen, untreated wood and basketware to enhance the charm of this look.

DIVIDING THE SPACE

The secret to the successful design of a dual-purpose room is to create enough of a physical division to define the two areas, while maintaining a uniformity of interior colour scheming between them. Depending on the different uses you wish to designate to each area, you may or may not wish to divide the room up into its two different functions. A sitting room/dining room does not really need to be segregated, although a shelf unit would make a useful divider. However, here the room is both a living room and a bedroom, so the two areas need to be easily separated – the dividing line is defined by the architecture of the room. Simply by screwing a long wooden curtain pole above the alcove, a full-length drape can be put up which, when not in use, is drawn to one side and held in place with a length of red and white ribbon. At night, when the area is to be divided temporarily, releasing the curtain neatly and instantly provides a private bedroom area, separated from the living room. Such a ploy would also work well in a large bedroom where you want to define a dressing-room 'space', or even to screen off a wash-basin or bathroom area. Keep an eye out for magazine articles that suggest clever and interesting ways to divide rooms. Cut out and stick on your sample board any particularly inspiring examples.

DUAL-PURPOSE FURNITURE

The second golden rule in successful one-room living is to use truly dual-purpose furniture wherever possible. This room, which is a sitting room by day and a bedroom by night, benefits from the neat solution of a day bed which resembles an elegant sofa for daytime lounging, but which becomes a divan at night. An alternative solution would be a sofa bed, but this is an expensive piece of furniture, and sofa beds are not designed to be slept in every night. Instead, you could easily and cheaply make a day bed for yourself by converting an existing divan. Start by screwing two matching end boards to the divan base, one at the

'foot' and one at the 'head' of the bed. You can use MDF board or cut square struts of MDF nailed together, as here. Your local timber merchant should be able to cut the MDF to your exact requirements. You can add more decoration if you wish. Here, the attractive, open-trellis design is topped by two wooden balls, glued in position using a glue gun. Once the divan has matching decorative ends, it will start to resemble an elegant day bed that will grace even the most formal sitting room. Complete the transformation by painting the MDF a coffee colour using oil-based eggshell paint.

The way in which you dress the bed is all-important if it is not going to look out of place in your daytime sitting room. Forget conventional rectangular pillows and duvets. Instead, dress the day bed with formal, matching bolsters at both ends and a pair of large, square cushions. Hide the divan itself beneath a fitted, square cover and matching valance. Choose matching – or at least co-ordinating – fabrics for all parts of the day bed, trying them out on your sample board first to confirm that they complement your other choices. That way the finished day bed will look smart enough to deceive visitors as to its humble origins. Then, at night, all you have to do is throw off the bolsters and cushions, and peel back the fitted cover to reveal your bed, made up with crisp, white cotton sheets.

STORAGE SPACE

As well as your bed, other pieces of furniture need to fit into the dual-purpose nature of your scheme. Extremely useful is the large, double-doored cupboard shown here. This is the perfect linen store for pillows during the day, and bolsters and fitted bed covers at night. The top of the cupboard provides a useful surface for accessories, storage boxes and baskets.

The cupboard used here has been given a decorative treatment so that it fits in perfectly with the room scheme. You can achieve a similar effect yourself: search in junk shops and second-hand furniture stores for a suitable piece. One of the most important things to bear in mind at this stage is the size of cupboard that your room can accommodate, especially if you have a particular alcove in mind where you wish to position it. Also, make sure that

Cream, coffee and two shades of red define this simple and sophisticated room scheme. If you stick to these colours your design should be successful.

A deep raspberry-red fabric remnant makes a useful purchase for cushion covers, lampshades, curtain trims or tie-backs.

Comfort is paramount: this cosy, upholstered armchair is home to a variety of decorative, designer cushions.

the cupboard is not too deep, or it may protrude too far into the room and take up valuable floor space. Once you have found a suitable cupboard, paint it with two coats of cream eggshell paint for a durable finish. Then, when dry, select a pale, coffee-coloured eggshell paint and 'wipe' this all over the cupboard with a clean, dry rag, using a circular motion. The darker paint will be deposited over the cream base to create an attractive, aged look.

To further enhance the period look of the linen cupboard, the door panels can be replaced, as here, with chicken wire before the cupboard is painted. You can get unusual ideas like this by looking round expensive antique furniture stores and noting down ideas. Pin the notes to your sample board to help

you transform your own junk-shop finds.

To add wire fronts to your cupboards, carefully cut away the central door panels from the surrounding frame, using a small saw. Rub the edges smooth with a medium-grade sandpaper.

Next, cut out a rectangular piece of chicken wire to a size slightly larger than the panel area, and attach this to the surrounding frame on the inside of the cupboard door using a heavy-duty upholstery staple gun. Repeat for the other door. Cut a rectangle of red and white patterned fabric to the same size as the chicken-wire panel and, pulling it taut, staple it neatly inside the door frame behind the wire, making sure that the fabric is straight. You can swop the fabric for another design if you want to co-ordinate the cupboard with another room scheme.

DECORATIVE CURTAINS

The curtain treatment in this room is both simple and elaborate at the same time. The simplicity lies in the choice of fabric which is a plain, coffee-coloured weave: alternatives include calico, hessian or linen. The elaborate effect comes from the design of the curtains and, fortunately, this is easily achieved using very economical fabrics, so do not stint on the lining. Curtains that are unlined never hang well or look very attractive, and, with such a plain, light-coloured fabric, the sunlight is apt to flood through.

Always use floor-length curtains for added elegance; somehow drapes that end at the window sill can look disappointingly utilitarian. To adorn the top of the curtain where it hangs from a dark wooden pole, coloured ribbon has been sewn on at intervals and tied into little bows. The leading edges of the curtains have been decorated with a strip of fabric to create an elaborate border that matches

Fringing and uphol-stery trims add style to a formal sitting room. Look out for sales bargains or discontinued rem-nants to use in your scheme.

the cupboard doors. This device is also very useful if you wish to increase the length and width of your curtains, when moving house, for instance. Simply sew an additional 'L' shape of fabric at the centre meeting edges and across the bottom of the curtains. If they are made from a patterned fabric, add on an 'L' shape of fabric in a plain, co-ordinating colour. Here, the drapes are combined with roller blinds made up in the same fabric as the curtain edging. Give plain roller blinds a prettier, softer look with a curved hem, highlighted with a frill. If money is tight, use the roller blinds for privacy and the drapes just as 'dress' curtains that cannot be drawn and which can therefore be made from just one fabric width or even less.

CREATIVE CANDELABRA

The wrought-iron candelabra hanging over the day bed adds a distinctive style to the room and helps to define the sleeping area.

 To achieve a similar effect, start by selecting as fine a candelabra as you

$\int$ EA-SHELL PICTURE

Pictures and paintings look wonderful on the walls of a sitting room or bedroom, but can be very expensive. It is very simple to create your own pic-ture using sea shells gathered from the shore. If you live too far from a beach to make this practi-cal you could do much the same using pieces of bark and cinna-mon sticks, or even leaves and seed pods.

STEP I

Take four equal lengths of wood or MDF and cut the ends to exactly 45° using a mitre block and a hacksaw.

can. Look for thin, curving metal arms rather than a sturdy, practical design. Then add ornate glass rings over the neck of each candle holder, to catch wax drips.

You can add to the elaborate decorative style of a candelabra by hanging clear glass jewel drops from the arms, securing them with wire. These will sparkle when the candles are lit.

Complete the effect, by wrapping a length of red and white striped ribbon around the hanging chain, finishing it off with a flamboyant, floppy bow tied just above the candelabra. Keep the ribbon well away from the lighted candles and never leave them unattended.

This idea can also be used to hide the electrical cable suspending a simple pendant light. Secure the ribbon at the top of the cable with a piece of double-sided tape then wind the ribbon round and round the wire, overlapping it to cover any gaps. At the bottom, secure with more adhesive tape. Then take a 30 cm (1 ft) length of matching ribbon and tie a bow at the top, trimming the ends to finish.

DESIGNS ON CUSHIONS

Cushions are particularly important in this dual-purpose bedroom/sitting room – where cushions and bolsters are used to dress the day bed. For these a wide deckchair stripe fabric was used, decorated with a transverse panel and large, tied bow. The bolsters were made of a co-ordinating red and white candy stripe with a cross-shaped bow at either end.

You can choose from a number of inexpensive fabrics to make cushions for this scheme: natural calico, sacking, hessian and ticking are all possibilities. You can have a lot of fun decorating a selection of cushions to pile up on your day bed or armchairs. Decorative ideas include making a circular cover from plain cream calico, which is then decorated with plain cord piping interspersed with raffia. On the front of the cushion you can sew a triangle of fabric-covered buttons. These can be highlighted by stitching on a circle of natural raffia.

Alternatively, wrap a square cushion in cream-coloured raw silk, just as you would a parcel, using tiny stitches to secure the 'wrapping'.

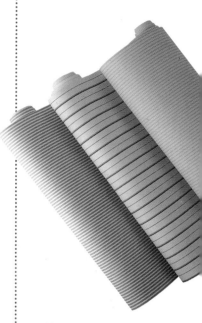

If you prefer wall-paper for a more formal atmosphere, these finely striped, ticking-style designs are just right for this dual-purpose room.

STEP 2

Assemble the frame by gluing the lengths together with a glue gun or strong wood adhesive, taking care to wipe away any excess glue.

STEP 3

Once the frame is assembled, paint it with two coats of vinyl matt emulsion and leave to dry.

STEP 4

Cut a piece of card into a rectangle to fit the frame. Cover the card with hessian and glue in place. Take care to keep the corners smooth by snipping away any excess fabric and gluing neatly on the reverse.

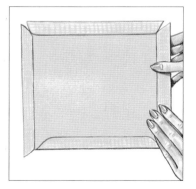

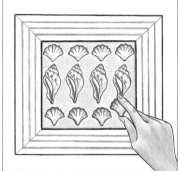

STEP 5

Tape the hessian-covered card to the edges of the frame, on the reverse side, using strong, self-adhesive tape.

STEP 6

Finally, glue a collection of sea shells to the hessian-covered card using a strong adhesive or glue gun. Screw two screwrings to the reverse of the frame and thread with string to hang the picture.

PHOTOGRAPHY

APPLE FRESH BEDROOM
Page 14/15: *Stylist – Siân Rees Photographer – Geoffrey Frosh © IPC MAGAZINES*
Page 19: *Stylist – Siân Rees Photographer – Geoffrey Frosh © IPC MAGAZINES*

NEW ENGLAND BEDROOM
Page 22/23: *Stylist – Judith Wilson Photographer – Graham Rae © IPC MAGAZINES*
Page 27: *Photographer – Martin Chaffer photo courtesy of Dulux Paints*

SUNSHINE DAYS BEDROOM
Page 30/31: *Stylist – Siân Rees Photographer – Chris Drake © IPC MAGAZINES*
Page 35: *Stylist – Siân Rees Photographer – Chris Drake © IPC MAGAZINES*

PAINTED TILE-EFFECT BATHROOM
Page 38/39: *Stylist – Siân Rees Photographer – Graham Rae © IPC MAGAZINES*
Page 43: *photo courtesy of Doulton Bathroom Products*

TULIP TIME BATHROOM
Page 47: *Stylist – Fiona Bourne Photographer – Lucinda Symons © IPC MAGAZINES*
Page 51: *Stylist – Fiona Bourne Photographer – Lucinda Symons © IPC MAGAZINES*

CITY SLICK BATHROOM
Page 55: *Stylist – Siân Rees Photographer – Chris Drake © IPC MAGAZINES*
Page 59: *Stylist – Siân Rees Photographer – Chris Drake © IPC MAGAZINES*

NATURAL CHOICE BATHROOM
Page 63: *Stylist – Fiona Bourne Photographer – Lucinda Symons © IPC MAGAZINES*
Page 67: *Stylist – Fiona Bourne Photographer – Lucinda Symons © IPC MAGAZINES*

PROVENÇAL STYLE KITCHEN
Page 70/71: *Stylist – Fiona Bourne Photographer – Tom Leighton © IPC MAGAZINES*
Page 75: *Stylist – Fiona Bourne Photographer – Tom Leighton © IPC MAGAZINES*

COUNTRY STYLE KITCHEN
Page 78/79: *Stylist – Alison Davidson Photographer – Trevor Richards © IPC MAGAZINES*
Page 83: *Stylist – Alison Davidson Photographer – Trevor Richards © IPC MAGAZINES*
Page 85: *Stylist – Alison Davidson Photographer – Trevor Richards © IPC MAGAZINES*

CARIBBEAN COLOUR KITCHEN
Page 86/87: *Stylist – Siân Rees Photographer – Lucinda Symons © IPC MAGAZINES*
Page 91: *Stylist – Siân Rees Photographer – Lucinda Symons © IPC MAGAZINES*

TURKISH DINING ROOM
Page 95: *Stylist – Siân Rees Photographer – Trevor Richards © IPC MAGAZINES*
Page 99: *Stylist – Siân Rees Photographer – Trevor Richards © IPC MAGAZINES*

DUAL-PURPOSE LIVING ROOM
Page 102/103: *Photographer – Chris Drake, Robert Harding Picture Library*
Page 107: *Photographer – Chris Drake, Robert Harding Picture Library*

GARDEN SITTING ROOM
Page 110/111: *Stylist – Judith Wilson Photographer – Chris Drake © IPC MAGAZINES*
Page 115: *Stylist – Judith Wilson Photographer – Chris Drake © IPC MAGAZINES*

SWEDISH STYLE STUDY
Page 118/119: *Stylist – Siân Rees Photographer– Lucinda Symons © IPC MAGAZINES*
Page 123: *Stylist – Siân Rees Photographer – Lucinda Symons © IPC MAGAZINES*

EASY LIVING ROOM
Page 126/127: *Stylist – Alison Davidson Photographer – Tim Imrie © IPC MAGAZINES*
Page 131: *Stylist – Alison Davidson Photographer – Pia Tryde © IPC MAGAZINES*

ONE-ROOM SPACE
Page 134/135: *Photographer – Jan Baldwin, Robert Harding Picture Library*
Page 139: *Photographer – Trevor Richards, Robert Harding Picture Library*

INDEX